H.J. CLARKE obtained his B.A. honours degree in history at University College, London before enlisting in H.M. Forces where his war service included secondment to the Personnel Selection Staff at the War Office. He has had wide experience of teaching and is now Head of the History Department of the Latymer School, Edmonton. He has acted as Schoolmaster-Moderator in A-level History for the London University Examining Board and as A-level Examiner in American History for the Southern Universities Joint Board.

KU-352-919

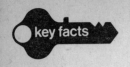

key facts

Reference Library

BIOLOGY, R. Whitaker, B.Sc., and
J. M. Kelly, B.Sc.

CHEMISTRY, K. Ahmad, M.A.

MATHEMATICS, K. Ahmad, M.A.

PHYSICS, K. Ahmad, M.A.

GEOGRAPHY, R. Knowles, M.A.

Key Facts Reference Library

GCE O-Level

HISTORY
1815–1914

by H.J. Clarke, B.A.

Published by Charles Letts & Co Ltd
London, Edinburgh and New York

First published 1978 by Intercontinental Book Productions

Published 1982 by Charles Letts & Co Ltd
Diary House, Borough Road, London SE1 1DW

1st edition   2nd impression
© Charles Letts & Co Ltd
Made and printed by Charles Letts (Scotland) Ltd
ISBN 0 85097 429 1

Contents

Introduction

This book is intended as a basic reference and revision book for O-level students of English History from 1815 to 1914 and for students of the new sixth form who are not taking the A-level examination.

Part 1 of the book gives a chronological survey of the major political events in English history, in the period. Part 2 selects significant social themes that have retained their appeal for today's students and develops them over the whole century that spans from the Napoleonic collapse to the outbreak of the First World War.

As far as the nature of the subject matter will allow, the book is designed as an easy reference book, with topics and key words in bold typescript, and as an aid to revision. For this purpose there is an index as well as a table of contents, so that the student may develop complete mastery of the essential detail of the course.

England After Napoleon

Lord Liverpool's Tory government were afraid of a revolution in this country. They continued Pitt's war-time Combination Acts and added further repressive laws which were designed to maintain law and order. Their economic policy did nothing to help the working classes and helped to provoke the very riots that the government wished to avoid. The many demands for reform finally led to a more liberal attitude that coincided with the death of Castlereagh, the Leader of the House of Commons, and the inclusion of new blood in the cabinet.

Government repression

The penal code and the game laws were very harsh, with transportation and even death as the punishment for trivial offences, as a deterrent to crime when there was no effective police force. Government spies were employed to mingle with the workers and so discover plots and identify agitators. **Habeas corpus** was suspended and the **Seditious Meetings Act** retained in 1817 in an attempt to silence such radicals as Hunt and Cobbett by arresting leaders and preventing public meetings.

The Six (Gag) Acts (1819) reinforced the government's powers by:
1. Empowering magistrates to search for arms.
2. Banning unauthorized military training.
3. Empowering magistrates to delay justice for misdemeanours.
4. Requiring a licence from a J.P. for meetings of fifty or more.
5. Punishing blasphemous and seditious libels.
6. Requiring a duty of fourpence on all pamphlets.

Economic policy

The Corn Law (1815) was passed by the government to prevent the wholsale bankruptcy of farmers who were finding it difficult to keep up mortgage payments in the face of renewed foreign competition. It forbade the import of foreign corn until English corn had reached a price of 80 shillings a quarter. Whilst this helped the farmer, it put an additional burden upon the workers by keeping the cost of bread high. **Income tax** which had been introduced as a war-time measure, was ended in 1816 so that the government had to raise extra revenue from indirect taxation, which fell heavily upon the working class and added to the cost of living.

Finance and trade which had been hampered by Napoleon's Berlin and Milan Decrees, was hindered by a mass of obsolete restrictions such as those imposed by the Navigation Acts. The enormous rise in the national debt and the distrust of our new paper currency meant the country's credit was not good.

The return to peace brought **unemployment** for demobilized soldiers and sailors and for workers supplying munitions, clothing etc., for the armed forces.

The policy of Laissez Faire meant that the government did nothing to improve the lot of the workers, although this doctrine did not prevent the continued ban on any attempt by the workers to combine in their efforts to obtain better pay and conditions from their employers. It meant, too, that the evils that had developed as a result of the industrial and agrarian revolutions continued, so that the stigma of pauperization remained for the farm labourer while long hours, low pay, bad conditions and periodic unemployment were the lot of the workers in the new towns.

Unrest and disorders

Denied any legal way of bringing their troubles to the notice of the government, the workers turned to acts of protest which were sometimes violent.

The Luddites, so called after their fictitious leader, Ned Ludd, smashed machinery in the belief that it was the cause of their unemployment. They were particularly active around Nottingham.

The Spa Field riot (1816), where there was a raid on a gunsmith's shop outside London, seemed to confirm government fears that an armed rebellion was contemplated.

The royal coach was stoned (1817). The royal family had rarely fallen lower in the esteem of their people, who were ashamed of their antics and in particular the Royal Divorce Bill.

The Blanketeers (1817), marched from Manchester, hoping to present their grievances in London. They got only as far as Derby, where their leaders were arrested.

Peterloo (1819) was the name given in derision to an affair in St. Peter's Fields, Manchester, where 'Orator' Hunt was speaking on such slogans as 'No Corn Laws', 'Equal Representation or Death'. The magistrates panicked and called in the military who charged the crowd and left casualties put at 11 killed and 500 wounded. The government congratulated the magistrates on their action.

The Cato Street Conspiracy was a plot, led by Thistlewood, who planned to blow up the cabinet at dinner. A government spy revealed the plot and the conspirators were executed.

Demands for reform

Demands for reform took many forms and came from many sections of society although usually voiced by the middle classes.
The penal code was very severe and yet was not acting as the deterrent that the government hoped. **Sir Samuel Romilly** and **Sir James Mackintosh** argued for less severe punishment.
Prison conditions were notoriously bad and were attacked by **John Howard** and **Elizabeth Fry**.
Slavery was regarded by some as a degrading institution for a civilized society and its abolition was urged by **William Wilberforce**, Clarkson and the Clapham sect. Britain's part in the Slave Trade had already been banned in 1807.
The Combination Laws, which denied workers the right to combine, were attacked by **Francis Place**.
Catholic emancipation had been promised to the Irish at the Act of Union (1801) and they clamoured for this under the leadership of **Daniel O'Connell** who worked peacefully for the rights of the Catholics as a step towards the setting up of an Irish parliament.
Parliamentary reform was the aim of many reformers who believed that if parliament could be made more representative of the nation then reform could come about peacefully. The Whigs, led by **Lord Grey** and **Lord John Russell**, had advocated this throughout their long term in opposition and they had support from many **radicals**, from the **Benthamites** and from **poets** such as Coleridge, Southey and Shelley.

Tory reformers

The suicide of Lord Castlereagh (1822) provided Lord Liverpool with the opportunity to bring new and more liberal men into his cabinet. The resulting reforms which were mainly administrative in character went some way towards quieting the clamour for reform and ending the disorders of the previous decade. Canning, the new Leader of the House of Commons, who was much more popular than his predecessor, personified the new spirit of mild reform.
Huskisson as the new President of the Board of Trade, supported by **Robinson** (later Lord Goderich) as Chancellor of the Exchequer implemented many ideas to ease the flow of trade and tighten the bonds of empire.

9

Free Trade measures, stemming from the ideas of Adam Smith's book *The Wealth of Nations* were introduced by the reduction and tidying up of import duties, by the signing of reciprocity treaties with nations such as the French and by a modifying of the Navigation Laws.

Bonds of Empire were strengthened by a system of preferential tariffs for empire goods and by the encouragement of emigration to the colonies by assisted passages.

The Corn Law was improved by the introduction of a sliding scale of tariffs designed to ease the fluctuation in corn prices brought about by the actions of unscrupulous traders.

Peel at the Home Office, took up the ideas of reformers and put them into practice.

Law and order was to be given a new image by several measures:

1. Benefit of Clergy was to be abolished.
2. The employment of government spies discontinued.
3. Prisons to be reformed, with prisons being inspected and the temptation for jailers to accept bribes being removed by higher pay and with women warders for women prisoners.
4. The penal code was reformed with the abolition of the death penalty for over 100 minor offences.
5. The death penalty was retained for only four offences.

Later (in 1829), Peel was to introduce his Metropolitan Police in an effort to make the certainty of being caught, the main deterrent to crime.

The repeal of the Combination Acts was due to the work of the radical **Place** and his M.P. friend **Hume**. They were able to convince the government that these laws tended to cause strikes by forbidding them. The laws were removed (1824) but had to be in part re-imposed (1825) because of more strikes.

Wellington's ministry

Wellington, with his ideas of loyalty to the crown and die-hard conservatism does not fit in neatly with other Tory Reformers but some important reforms were passed during his ministry:

The Corn Law was again modified (1828) by the introduction of a new sliding scale.

The Test and Corporation Acts were repealed in 1828 so that Nonconformists could hold government and municipal offices without the need for an annual indemnity act.

The Catholic Relief Act was now difficult to postpone. O'Connell by winning the County Clare election, made Wellington and Peel afraid that revolution would follow in Ireland if he were not able to take his seat. Peel, loyally, stood by Wellington to enable the Catholic Relief Act to be passed and so allow O'Connell to sit in the House of Commons.

Metropolitan Police were set up in 1829 for the London Area. It was so successful that other parts of the country set up similar forces under the control of Watch Committees.

Foreign policy

The government's foreign policy was directed by Castlereagh until his death in 1822. His success in maintaining the Quadrupal Alliance against Napoleon until the latter's defeat in 1815, made Castlereagh well known in Europe and expert in diplomacy by congress.

At the Congress of Vienna (1815), Castlereagh:
1. Ensured that the treatment of France was not vindictive.
2. Resisted the developing might of Russia and Prussia.
3. Gained valuable lands for Britain in the colonial field.
4. Preferred the Quadrupal Alliance to the Holy Alliance.

Congress of Aix la Chapelle was attended by Castlereagh. It was the first and most successful of the meetings of the Congress System. It re-admitted France as one of the powers and withdrew the army of occupation from France as well as agreeing on some minor proposals e.g., N. African slave trade.

At Troppau and Laibach (1820 & 1821), Castlereagh opposed the general right of the powers to intervene in the internal affairs of countries to put down revolutions and so preserve peace. He did, however, agree to this in specific areas where the power had some special interest e.g. Austria in Italy.

In the U.S.A., he successfully negotiated that:
1. The rival navies on the Great Lakes should be banned.
2. That the 49th parallel be recognized as the boundary between Canada and the U.S.A. from the Great Lakes to the Rocky Mountains.
3. That Oregon should be administered jointly.

Canning took over the Foreign Office in 1822. He championed liberal governments abroad and gained influence for Britain with those governments. He:
1. Broke with the other powers at the **Congress of Verona**.
2. Opposed the return of the **S.American republics** to Spain and furthered British trade there.
3. Supported the liberal regime in **Portugal** and gained influence there and in **Brazil**.
4. Obtained partial independence for **Greece** (Treaty of London). Safeguarded British trade with the Greeks.

England Under the Whigs

When Lord Grey took office in 1830, he was prepared and expected to introduce parliamentary reform. The bill did not pass without a struggle but its passage marked an important era of reform carried out partly under Lord Grey and partly under Lord Melbourne.

The old parliamentary system

The old system had become out of date in many respects and did not represent nineteenth century England.

The constituencies were unequal in size. All **counties** sent two members to parliament regardless of their size (with the exception of Yorkshire which in 1821, took over the two seats of Grampound, a borough disfranchised on account of corruption). All **boroughs** also sent two members although some had flourished and some had declined.

70% of members represented constituencies south of a line from the Bristol Channel to the Wash, whilst the royal duchy of Cornwall sent 44 members as opposed to 45 for the whole of Scotland. The drift of population to the new Lancashire cotton towns had not been accompanied by any change in the constituencies.

The qualification for the vote varied enormously. In **county** constituencies, there was a uniform qualification—the 40 shilling freeholder. In the **boroughs**, the qualification varied according to local custom:

1. **Potwalloper** boroughs where anyone renting a room where a pot could be boiled had a vote were quite democratic.
2. Boroughs where the vote went to householders paying '**scot and lot**' were less democratic.
3. **Burgage** boroughs, where the vote went to the owners of certain properties, had a narrow franchise.
4. In **Corporation** Boroughs, the vote went only to members of the corporation.
5. In **Freeman** Boroughs, the vote went only to freemen of the borough.

Only 435 000 out of a population of 13 000 000 had the vote.

Elections were often corrupt. Electors, especially in rotten boroughs, could sell their vote; owners of pocket boroughs sold seats to the highest bidder. Open voting at hustings made it all too easy for electors to be bribed or intimidated.

The landed gentry dominated not only the House of Lords but also the House of Commons. The county electors tended to be influenced by the local landowner. In pocket boroughs, the patron chose the member. In rotten boroughs the voters could often be influenced by intimidation or bribery.

Arguments were put forward **in favour of the old system:**
1. It worked well.
2. It enabled us to withstand Napolean.
3. It was the envy of the world. Montesquieu praised it in *L'Esprit des Lois*. The Founding Fathers imitated it when they drew up the American constitution.
4. It enabled young men of ability, e.g. the Younger Pitt, to come to the fore at an early age.

The struggle to pass the bill

The Committee on Parliamentary Reform set up by the government under the chairmanship of Lord Durham recommended:
1. The disfranchisement of decayed towns.
2. The enfranchisement of large new towns.
3. A uniform franchise for borough constituencies.

This could mean that many sitting members would lose their seat and it proved to be a real struggle to pass the bill.

The first bill (March 1831) passed its second reading in the House of Commons but was defeated in the committee stage and the subsequent general election gave the Whigs a greater majority.

The second bill (June 1831) passed the Commons, only to be rejected by the Lords. This defeat was followed by rioting in the country as the mob demonstrated its support for the bill.

The third bill (December 1831) passed the Commons but was made unrecognisable by amendments in the Lords. This was followed by demonstrations, such as, 'The bill, the whole bill and nothing but the bill'. Lord Grey was able to obtain the king's promise to create enough peers to pass the bill and this encouraged 100 peers, led by Wellington, to abstain. The bill received the royal assent in June 1832.

The terms of the act

The right to vote was kept by the 40 shilling freeholder in the **county** constituencies, while the £10 per annum copyholder and the £50 short leaseholder were given the vote. In the **boroughs**, a new uniform qualification, the £10 per annum householder, was agreed.

Constituencies were changed in two ways:

1. Small boroughs (rotten and pocket boroughs) lost seats: where the population was under 2 000 the borough was disfranchised and where the population was between 2 000 and 4 000 the borough lost one seat. In this way 143 seats were available for redistribution.

2. These seats were given to large counties, industrial towns, Scotland and Ireland.

Results of the act

Gradually, the landowners, found that their influence was being challenged by the **middle classes**, who now had the vote and began to appear in parliament.

The **workers** were very disappointed that they did not receive the vote (in some cases, they lost it). Neither parliamentary party seemed to offer them any hope: for **Russell** the act was final and he was nicknamed 'Finality Jack'; **Peel** as the Tory leader held no hope for the workers. They turned to movements such as Owen's **Grand National Consolidated Trades Union** and to **Chartism**.

The act did nothing to lessen corruption but it was looked upon as a first step towards democracy and it did lead the way to an era of reform.

Later Whig reforms

Slavery still existed in the British Empire, mainly in the West Indies and South Africa. This was abolished in 1833 following the work of **Wilberforce**, Clarkson and the Clapham Sect. Slave owners were compensated for the loss of their slaves at about £38 per slave with the government finding £20 000 000 for the purpose. The **West Indian slaves** were to serve as apprentices to their former masters as a halfway stage to freedom but the sugar trade never recovered from this and unemployment became widespread.

In Cape Colony the **Boers** were not prepared to accept abolition and in 1835 they went on to the **Great Trek** and established the republics of Transvaal and Orange Free State.

The Factory Act (1833) banned the employment of children under 9 years in factories. Children aged 9 to 13 could work a nine hour day, whilst young people from 13 to 18 were limited to a 12 hour day. Children under 13 were to attend school for two hours a day. Unlike earlier acts, this appointed paid inspectors to enforce the regulations.

A £20 000 grant for education, voted in 1833, was to be shared between the Church of England (National) schools and the Nonconformist (Lancasterian) schools. This established the principle of state involvement in Education.

The Poor Law Amendment Act (1834) was a Benthamite measure which tried to rationalize the poor law by eliminating the waste and corruption under the Speenhamland system. **Outdoor relief** was abolished for the able bodied, who now had to enter one of the new **workhouses** set up by unions of parishes, to obtain relief. The scheme was to be run by three Commissioners in London, with the aid of **Edwin Chadwick** as secretary and local **Boards of Guardians**, elected locally. The scheme meant ten years of hardship for the working classes and the workhouses became hated and feared for the harshness of life inside: it did, however, cut down the burden on the rates and end the pauperization of the working class.

The Municipal Corporations Act (1835) ended the closed and often corrupt corporations in English towns. The **ratepayers** were to elect **councillors** for three years; councillors elected **aldermen** for six years (for continuity); councillors and aldermen elected a **mayor** for one year. The accounts had to be audited annually, and they gradually took over the work of Improvement Commissions. They also had the right to levy rates.

Registration of births, marriages and deaths was made compulsory in 1836. This made it possible to keep more accurate statistics and to enforce the provisions of the 1833 Factory Act.

Penny post (1840) was the idea of Rowland Hill, a Post Official, who considered the old system wasteful of the postman's time and to involve unnecessary book-keeping. There was to be a charge of 1 penny, payable in advance by means of a stamp, for letters up to $\frac{1}{2}$ oz, regardless of distance. The **penny black stamp** was introduced for this purpose. It ran at a loss for 23 years but led to a great increase in letter writing both for business and for pleasure. Eventually the increase in business meant that a profit was made and the charge remained at 1 penny until the First World War.

Climbing boys (1840) were employed to sweep chimneys by climbing up inside them. Cases of death by suffocation or eventual consumption led the government, after agitation from Lord Shaftesbury, to ban the apprenticeship of boys under sixteen for this purpose.

Tithe Commutation Act (1840) put an end to the long quarrel over the payment of a tithe or tenth to the clergy, by changing the tithe into an additional rent, payable in money.

The working classes

The impressive record of the Whigs as regards reforms failed to endear them to the working classes. Their efforts to improve living conditions met with a reaction reminiscent of that of the Tories after 1815.

The Labourers' Revolt (1830–31) is the name given to the spontaneous rioting of farm workers in the southern and eastern counties where ricks were burnt, overseers of the poor ducked in village ponds and demands put forward for higher wages, lower rents and better poor relief. A special commission of judges hanged nine men or boys and transported or imprisoned hundreds of others.

The Reform Act (1832) did nothing for the workers and Lord John Russell made it plain that the Whigs did not intend to enfranchise the working classes, gaining the label of 'Finality Jack' for stating that the 1832 Act was final.

Trade unions were legalized in 1824 but the government were very alarmed by the growth of Robert Owen's Grand National Consolidated Trades Union which catered for all trades within one union with the ultimate possibility of a general strike as a weapon. The government struck at six men from Dorset (**The Tolpuddle Martyrs**), who were prosecuted for taking illegal oaths. In 1834, the six men were sentenced to seven years' transportation. The case resulted in a monster petition which forced the government to pardon and bring home the men. However, the trade union was discredited and the workers turned to other movements.

The Chartist movement began in 1836 with the London Working Men's Association. **William Lovett**, the secretary and **Francis Place**, who acted as an adviser, drew up a petition in the form of a bill, which had six points and which became known as the '**People's Charter**'. A convention to present the Charter to parliament was called for 1839, but the rejection of the petition by parliament caused a split in the ranks with Feargus O'Conner taking over the leadership of the more active 'Physical Force' Chartists.

The Anti-Corn Law League attracted much working class as well as middle class support with its promise of cheaper bread. It was formed in 1839 but its real impact came in Peel's ministry when, together with the Irish potato famine, it led to the repeal of the Corn Law and the downfall of Peel.

Friendly Societies had developed when trade union activity was difficult. In this period the main feature of the movement was the growth of Working Men's Orders and the connection of the movement with temperance. The societies had as their natural economic complement, the Savings Bank.

Foreign policy

Lord Palmerston had been Secretary at War under a succession of Tory Prime Ministers from 1809 to 1828. He was regarded more as a man about town than a serious politician until Grey offered him the Foreign Office in 1830. He came to be regarded as the expert on foreign affairs until his death in 1865.

Belgium had been united with Holland in 1815, under the Dutch king but differences of race, religion and language let to a demand for Belgian independence in 1830. Since Russia, Prussia and Austria were preoccupied with Poland and Louis Philippe was anxious for British goodwill, Palmerston took the initiative. Sending the British fleet to the Scheldt and using the French army, he prevailed upon the Dutch to accept **Belgian independence** and the French to forgo any territorial claims. After patient negotiation, an independent Belgium, with Leopold of Saxe Coburg as king, was accepted by the Belgians and guaranteed by all the powers.

The Polish Rising (1830) concerned all the Eastern powers, but the Poles were ruthlessly suppressed by Russia. All Palmerston could do was to protest and this was ignored. Palmerston was left suspicious of Russia henceforth and hostile to her expansion.

Spain and Portugal experienced similar conflicts between a young liberal queen and reactionary uncle. In Spain, **Don Carlos**, who enjoyed the support of Russia, Prussia and Austria was defeated with the help of British volunteers and the French Foreign Legion. In Portugal, Captain Napier R.N., took command of the Portuguese navy and destroyed **Dom Miguel's** fleet off Cape St. Vincent, while Queen Maria's army, with British volunteers, defeated his army.

The Eastern Question became important when **Mehemet Ali**, failing to get Crete and Syria as a reward for helping the Sultan, sent his son **Ibrahim** (1831) to invade Syria. He overran the area and threatened Constantinople and was only stopped when the Sultan accepted Russian help by the **Treaty of Unkiar Skelessi**. This treaty contained a secret clause giving Russia virtual control of the Dardanelles. This was a diplomatic triumph for Russia. The Sultan's attack (1839) on

Ibrahim and his defeat by land and sea aroused Russia's fear of a strong Moslem state in the area. Palmerston gained Russian co-operation in restricting Mehemet Ali to Egypt, against the wish of France by the **Treaty of London** (1841). Further a clause known as the **Straits Convention** reversed Russian rights over the Dardanelles and closed them to the warships of all nations in time of peace. This was a diplomatic victory for Palmerston over both Russia and France.

The Far East was the scene of more aggressive action by Britain. The Chinese government was anxious to prevent the smuggling of opium into the country. They rough-handled British merchants, seized their opium and prohibited trade with Britain. British merchants were keen to trade with China and Palmerston took a strong line. His demands on the Chinese led to the **First Opium War** (1840–42), with the British fleet bombarding Canton and thus forcing the Chinese to agree to the Treaty of Nanking, which was completed in Peel's ministry. By it Britain gained the lease of Hong Kong, the opening of five treaty ports to British trade and a start for Britain in the development of China.

Afghanistan became the scene of another war. Auckland, to keep Russian influence out of Afghanistan, decided to depose the Amir, Dost Mohammed, and replace him by a British puppet, Shah Suja, whose unpopularity was increased by his British connection. A rising in support of Dost Mohammed saw the death of several British and the slaughter of the Resident's troops as they were being evacuated. A relieving force found one survivor, sacked Kabul and then retreated. This **First Afghan War** had cost £15 000 000, seen an army of 15 000 destroyed and achieved nothing.

Aden became a British protectorate in 1839, when its ruler sought help against the expansionist tendencies of Mehemet Ali.

Peel and Conservatism

When Peel became Prime Minister in 1841 with a working majority, he had already announced his policies to the electors of what had been his father's constituency in his famous **Tamworth Manifesto**. He had sought to give the Tory Party a new image, by re-naming it the Conservative Party. He accepted the 1832 Reform Act but had no plans to extend the franchise to the workers. He promised to establish sound finance, as befitted the chairman of the Bullion Committee. He appealed for the support of the manufacturers and he promised cautious reform. These reforms were to be in the field of finance and trade and to a lesser extent in industry.

Finance and trade

Peel saw that the ending of income tax in 1815 had resulted in a host of customs duties on every day necessities. Huskisson had tried to bring order to these duties but many remained in 1841 and they had the result of putting articles such as tea, sugar, butter and soap out of the reach of the working classes. The duties also encouraged smuggling which was made profitable by the heavy duties. Most important of all, they hampered trade and by reducing our imports, cut down the amount of goods that other countries could buy from us. Peel decided that the free trade ideas of Adam Smith could provide the answer to many of Britain's problems in the 'hungry forties'.

Peel's 1842 budget set up a new system of tariffs whereby raw materials paid a maximum duty of 5%, so that British manufacture should have the benefit of cheap raw materials. Semi-manufactured goods paid a duty of 12% and manufactured goods paid 20%. In effect this gave some protection to our manufacturers who were expected to create new wealth for the country. Existing tariffs on a high percentage of articles in common use had to be reduced in order to comply with the new system and so goods became cheap for the consumer. It was expected that an increased volume of trade would follow, but to make up for the government's temporary loss of revenue, **income tax** was introduced at 7 pence in the £1, on incomes over £150 per annum.

Peel's 1845 budget removed the duty on a large number of further items imported and ended the duty on all exports. This step towards free trade was advantageous to Britain as a manufacturing country that needed to sell its goods abroad.

Peel also took the step of retaining income tax as a permanent feature in order to provide the money for campaigns in China and India which had been a legacy of the previous government.

The Corn Law was still causing fluctuations in the price of bread and Peel determined to improve the sliding scale. While keeping protection in time of plenty and free import in times of scarcity, he took the opportunity to lower the duty throughout the scale. Peel's sliding scale was a great improvement but demands were being raised for the total repeal of the Corn Law.

The Bank Charter Act (1844) was intended to prevent banks from lending large sums of money, really beyond their means, for the purpose of financing schemes such as the railway development. The act divided the Bank of England into two. The first carried on the ordinary banking business, the second controlled the issue of notes. New banks were forbidden to issue notes while the Bank of England had to have all notes over and above the fiduciary issue of £14 000 000 backed by bullion. The act helped to secure the stability of British banking which was essential to Britain's world wide trade.

The National Debt stood at £250 000 000. Peel lowered the rate of interest and thereby saved the Treasury a sum of £1 000 000 per annum.

Industry

The Mines Act (1842) Ashley (later Lord Shaftesbury) had been able to persuade the Whigs in 1840 to appoint a commission to study child employment in the mines. When it reported it showed such evil conditions in the mines for boys and girls that Ashley tried to ban all female labour in the mines as well as that of boys under thirteen. In the Lords the bill was amended so that the age limit for boys was ten. The act was to be strictly enforced by paid inspectors.

The Factory Act (1844) introduced a twelve hour day for women but the lower age group for children in factories was dropped to eight instead of nine. However, their hours were to be only six and a half per day instead of nine. They also had to have schooling. Ashley's agitation for a ten hour day was blocked by Peel. Safety regulations made their first appearance, in that children, young persons and women were prohibited from cleaning machinery whilst it was in motion.

The Railway Passengers Act (Cheap Trains Act) (1844) postponed a decision on nationalization of the railways and contented itself with providing that there must be at least one train per day, each way, at the third class fare of 1 penny per mile. This period saw the beginning of railway mania and the process of amalgamation that reduced the number of companies finally to four.

Ireland

O'Connell planned a mass meeting at Clontarf, in 1842 to frighten Peel into repealing the Act of Union, just as Wellington had been frightened over Catholic Emancipation. However when Peel banned the meeting, O'Connell, who believed in constitutional methods, called the meeting off and so lost the leadership to more extreme members of 'Young Ireland'.

The Maynooth grant was a grant to Maynooth College which trained Catholic priests. It shows that Peel was prepared to make concessions in combination with his firmness.

Queen's colleges were also established by Peel. They were nondenominational and represented an attempt to bring Catholics and Protestants together. The attempt failed and the colleges were dubbed as 'Godless' by both sides.

The potato blight (1845) meant that many of the Irish were faced with famine because potatoes were the staple diet of the poor. Peel was faced with a crisis and had to stand by and watch the Irish die or take action. The action which many people were demanding was the repeal of the Corn Law, so that cheap corn could be imported into Ireland.

The repeal of the Corn Law

Not only was Peel under pressure from the Irish famine to repeal the Corn Law, a powerful pressure group was also urging repeal.

The Anti-Corn Law League was founded in 1839 to force the repeal of the Corn Law and so enable foreign countries to sell us more of their corn. This would enable them to buy more of our manufactured goods. The leaders, Richard Cobden and John Bright were both M.Ps., the former provided the statistics for their campaign whilst the latter was a brilliant orator. Their promise of more trade attracted the wealthy middle classes and their promise of cheaper bread attracted the workers. Peel believed in Free Trade, but as leader of the party of landowners and also farmers, he needed time to educate his party.

The Edinburgh Letter was a demand for action by the government, issued by Lord John Russell, leader of the opposition. It had the effect of causing Peel to resign so that the Whigs could take office and carry the repeal. The Whigs, however, were just as divided as the Conservatives and Lord John was unable to form a cabinet; he handed back 'the poisoned chalice'.

The split in the Conservative Party was caused when Peel returned to office to carry through the repeal. Disraeli and Lord George Bentinck led the protectionist Tory back benchers against their own leader. The government carried the repeal and imported cheap American maize to ease the famine in Ireland, but their opponents defeated the government on a bill to take emergency powers to deal with unrest in Ireland. As a result the party was split into Conservatives, under Disraeli and Peelites, led by Peel. There was no Conservative government with a majority in the House for nearly 30 years.

Foreign policy

The first task of Peel's foreign secretary, Lord Aberdeen, was to end the legacy of trouble in China and Afghanistan that had been left by the previous government. There was also a crisis to be dealt with in America.

The U.S.-Canadian boundary had never been clearly defined at the ends, either from the Rocky Mountains to the Pacific Ocean or, in the East between Maine and New Brunswick.

The quarrel in the East was successfully settled by Lord Ashburton and his American counterpart, Webster. Both men were bankers and they produced the **Ashburton-Webster Agreement** which defined the disputed boundary.

The Oregon boundary, previously undefined, now became the cause of tension between the U.S.A. and Britain. President Polk put forward the claim to territory as far as the line of latitude 54°40′ in his election slogan 'Fifty four-forty or fight'. The British wanted the 49th parallel as the boundary. Agreement was finally reached by the **Oregon Treaty** which accepted the 49th parallel, with a small deviation to allow Britain to retain Vancouver Island.

Anglo-French entente was established by Lord Aberdeen who managed to restore the good relations between the two countries which had been upset by the restriction of Mehemet Ali to Egypt. The new relationship was cemented by a visit of Queen Victoria and Prince Albert to France (1843). The strength of the new entente was tested by a dispute over France's annexation of **Tahiti** and by the **Spanish Marriage** question. In both cases, a sensible approach to the question led to peaceful solution and the entente was upheld.

The Age of Palmerston

For almost twenty years (1846–1865), Palmerston dominated the politics of the country. He was rarely out of high office; he served as Foreign Secretary (1846–51), Home Secretary (1852–55), Prime Minister (1855–58 and 1859–65). Palmerston might have founded a great progressive party, but he was not interested in parliamentary reform which was the great issue of the day. His interests lay in foreign affairs and he was in a position to use Britain's wealth and influence almost as he wished.

Foreign Secretary (1846–51)

Anglo-French relations took a turn for the worse, when Louis Philippe, not feeling bound by an arrangement reached with Peel's government, arranged for the marriage of his son (Duc de Montpensier) to the younger sister of the Queen of Spain and that of Don Francis, a cousin, to the queen. Since Don Francis was not thought capable of having children, this could have led to a French prince claiming the throne of Spain. This ended the entente and as it turned out the French prince did not succeed in Spain.

In Switzerland (1847) Palmerston intervened to support the Swiss Confederation when the Sonderbund (Catholic Conservative Cantons) were trying to secede, with the support of Louis Philippe. The Confederation was maintained with what Palmerston regarded as a victory for constitutionalism.

Italy, in 1847, was anxious to gain independence and Palmerston believed that the collapse of Austria was imminent. He sent Lord Minto on a mission to fortify the Italian liberals and sent arms from Woolwich arsenal. He was bitterly disappointed when Austria regained her position and was even more prejudiced towards Austria. He supported the Sultan's refusal to surrender Kossuth and later received Kossuth and snubbed Haynau.

Don Pacifico was a Portuguese money lender, who having been born in Gibraltar, was able to claim British citizenship. When his house in Athens was pillaged and his claim for compensation ignored by the Greek government, he appealed to the Foreign Office. Palmerston took the matter up (1850) and ordered a naval blockade of Greek ports. There were strong protests from Russia and France, who were guarantors of Greek independence and from the House of Commons.

Palmerston, however, in a $4\frac{1}{2}$ hour speech was able to defend himself by saying that a British citizen should be entitled to the support of his government by pleading 'civis Britannicus sum', just as St. Paul had been able to say 'civis Romanus sum'. The whole episode merely enhanced Palmerston's popularity. **His dismissal** came about because his prejudice against Austria and his refusal to consult the queen, met with her disapproval. When in December 1851, Palmerston expressed to the French ambassador, his approval of Louis Napoleon's coup, without informing the crown or the cabinet, Russell insisted upon his resignation. However as a private M.P., Palmerston was able to bring down the government in 1852, in his 'tit for tat on Johnny Russell'.

Home Secratary (1852–55)

Britain in 1851 had been the setting for the **Great Exhibition**. The conception and execution was carried through by the Prince Consort. The huge iron and glass structure in Hyde Park was the work of Joseph Paxton. Here, between May and October, more than six million visitors came to view the amazing variety of exhibits, tangible proof of the benefits of free trade. It was a staggering symbol of Britain's prosperity, so successful that it was agreed to re-elect this Crystal Palace, as it was called, in South London, where it remained until destroyed by fire in 1936. Lord Palmerston's period in the Home Office was not of any consequence apart from his opposition to parliamentary reform: it was Gladstone as Chancellor of the Exchequer who took a further step along the road to free trade in his **1853 budget**. This ended many tariffs on semi-manufactured goods and foodstuffs and halved the duty on manufactured goods.

Meanwhile the coalition of Peelites and Whigs under the Lords Aberdeen and Russell, blundered into the **Crimean War**. It was the feeble prosecution of the war that led to a public demand for Palmerston to become Prime Minister and to instil some vigour into the war effort.

Prime Minister (1855–58)

The causes of the Crimean War are trifling from the British point of view. The divisions in the cabinet prevented a clear policy from emerging and encouraged both Russians and Turks to expect Britain's goodwill or help. Both Russell and Palmerston were anxious to prevent any Russian expansion in the area and to safeguard our trade there. It would seem to

have been an unnecessary war from the British point of view.
The main events may be stated quite briefly:

The sinking of the Turkish fleet off **Sinope**, by the Russians was the signal for an allied attack on the Russian naval base of Sebastopol.

A landing was effected at **Eupatoria** and a Russian Force defeated at the **River Alma**.

The attack on Sebastopol was delayed until a full scale **siege** was necessary (due to Allied incompetence).

A series of Russian sorties were contained at the famous battles of **Balaclava, Inkerman** and **Tchernaya**.

Allied attacks on redoubts such as **Redan** were beaten off.

Russell's despatches to the Times revealed incompetence.

M. Soyer, a French chef, invented the Soyer stove to provide hot food for the troops.

The Tsar boasted of his great generals '**Janvier**' and '**Fevrier**', but the latter 'turned traitor' and killed the Tsar.

Florence Nightingale and her nurses brought comfort and cleanliness to the troops in the base hospital at Scutari.

Sebastopol fell in 1855.

A change of leadership in Britain and Russia helped bring about a truce.

The Treaty of Paris (1856)

In the Balkans, Moldavia and Wallachia became virtually independent and soon united to form Rumania.

The maintenance of warships and naval establishments on the Black Sea was forbidden (Russia broke this clause in 1870).

Russia renounced her right to protect Christians in Turkey and the Turks promised to behave better towards them.

Turkey remained intact (a buffer between Russia and the Mediterranean Sea).

The Arrow was a ship, which flew the British flag. It was not entitled to do so as its licence had expired. In 1857, it was caught whilst engaged in smuggling and piracy. But Palmerston took up the case and a British fleet fired on some forts near Canton to force a Chinese apology. Following a successful vote of censure on Palmerston, in the House, the people re-instated him in the 'Canton election'. Further demands on China led to an anglo-French expedition against Peking. Finally, the Chinese agreed to the **Treaty of Tientsin**, by which China agreed to allow the import of opium; to admit foreign ambassadors; to open more ports (including Tientsin) to trade; to recognize British officials. This is sometimes known as the Second Opium War.

The Indian Mutiny (1857) was put down vigorously but as a result of the horrors that occurred Palmerston decided to end the rule of the East India Company and bring the sub-continent under direct government rule. Before this could be done the government fell and the reorganization of the Indian government was left to the Conservatives.

The Conspiracy to Murder Bill caused the government's downfall. Following Orsini's attempt on the life of Napoleon III, and the subsequent representations by the French, the hatching of plots, in Britain, by exiles was made a felony. It was rejected by parliament and Palmerston resigned.

Prime Minister again (1859–65)

Once again Palmerston's main concern was with foreign affairs.

Benevolent neutrality towards Piedmont (1860–61) was consistent with the earlier attitude of Palmerston and Russell towards Italy. The presence of the British fleet facilitated the landing of the 'Thousand' in Sicily and its crossing to the mainland. Russell sent despatches to warn off any power from intervening. The support for Garibaldi was not shared by France.

The expedition to Mexico was arranged in conjunction with France and Spain in order to secure payment of interest on loans. When it was successfully completed, Palmerston, unlike Napoleon III, had the good sense to withdraw (1861–62).

His attitude to Denmark (1863–64) has attracted criticism. When war was imminent between Denmark and the Germanic confederation Palmerston tried to avert war by his famous statement, 'If Denmark fights, she will not fight alone'. Since Bismark recognized this for bluff, he ignored it; the war went on and no British action was taken.

Relations with the U.S.A. became very grave. On two occasions, during the American Civil War, ships caused problems for the two governments.

The 'Trent' a British ship was stopped (1861) by a Northern ship and two confederate envoys, Slidell and Mason, were taken off. This was a violation of Britain's neutrality and a strongly worded protest was drafted. The Prince Consort moderated the tone of the despatch and Lincoln released the envoys, averting the crisis.

The 'Alabama', built in Birkenhead, was allowed to join the South as a war ship. The ship caused considerable damage to Northern shipping. Russell refused to acknowledge any breach of neutrality and bad feeling remained till Gladstone settled the claim.

Domestic affairs played a minor part in Palmerston's second term as Prime Minister, but some important developments were going on. Steps were taken to complete free trade.

Gladstone's budget (1860) removed virtually all tariffs, leaving only twenty, which were retained for purposes of revenue.

The Cobden-Chevalier Treaty (1860) was a free trade treaty with France, whereby Britain admitted French wines and silks free of duty, while France admitted British manufactured goods on the same terms. This led to a big increase in trade between the two countries and led to a lessening of the tension which had been growing between them. The French manufacturers were unhappy about the scheme.

The paper tax was repealed (1861). These changes left Britain virtually a free trade country by 1865.

Working class movements

Little was done by the government to help the workers during the Age of Palmerston and many acted upon the ideas of Samuel Smiles in his book '*Self Help*'.

The Chartists were active again in 1848 (the year of revolutions). O'Connor planned a mass meeting at Kennington Common, to be the signal for a march to parliament to present a monster petition. O'Connor claimed to have six million signatures. The rain on the day and the preparations of Wellington kept the attendance down to 25 000 and O'Connor took the petition to Westminster in a cab. When it was found that many signatures were forged and that the total was nothing like six million, Chartism perished in the outburst of ridicule.

Trade unions formed unions of skilled workers along the lines of the Amalgamated Society of Engineers (1851). They became known as model unions and they concentrated on improving their rights and improving their security by means of an expensive fee. Their leaders, known as the Junta, tried to avoid violence. The First Trades Union Congress met in 1868 and formed a national body to unite the various unions.

The Rochdale Pioneers (1844) launched a consumers' co-operative by distributing their profits to the members by a dividend shareout. This has developed into the modern Co-operative movement.

Thrift continued to be popular and the Friendly Societies were able to prosper. Life insurance developed from this with the Prudential Society being formed in 1848 while the government set up the Post Office Savings Bank in 1861.

Truck gradually disappeared as a result of a campaign in 1850.

Gladstone and Disraeli

For some twenty years after the death of Palmerston, English politics were dominated by Gladstone and Disraeli. Gladstone drew together the Peelites, the Whigs and the Radicals to form the new Liberal Party, while Disraeli nursed the Conservative Party after its disastrous split and tried to develop a tie between those who governed and the working classes in what has been called a Tory Democracy. Disraeli was the first to become Prime Minister.

Disraeli's early career

Disraeli was not a typical Conservative. He was not an aristocrat, but a Jew. He was not educated at public school and one of the universities, but was self educated. He tried several careers; Law, Writing and Radical politics but met with little financial success.

In 1837, he became Conservative M.P. for Maidstone with two ideas, seemingly incompatible, that remained with him throughout his whole career. They were that action must be taken to help the workers and that the aristocracy were the natural leaders of the country. His eventual rise in the party was slow but was helped by three things. He married a wealthy widow who supported him in his political ambitions. He became the leader of the 'Young England' group in parliament. He and Bentinck led the protectionists in the Commons against Peel.

Derby-Disraeli ministries now followed with Disraeli as Leader of the House of Commons and Chancellor of the Exchequer but with the aging Lord Derby as the party's titular head and Prime Minister. Without a majority in the Commons, these ministries were limited as to what they could achieve:

The first Derby-Disraeli ministry had to face the fact that there was no future in opposing free trade and so they declared their support for it (1852).

The second Derby-Disraeli ministry reformed the Government of India after the Mutiny, with the East India Company coming to an end and the posts in the Indian Civil Service being filled by open competition, in place of patronage. Minor changes were made in parliamentary representation, with Jews being allowed in parliament and the property qualification for M.Ps. ending. The attempt to increase plural voting by a 'fancy franchise' failed.

The third Derby-Disraeli ministry passed a **Factory Act** (1867), which extended the scope of the factory acts to all trades as well as the **British North America Act** which established the Dominion of Canada as a Federal state, originally comprising Quebec, Ontario, Nova Scotia and New Brunswick. The act also allowed for the future expansion of the Dominion. Undoubtedly its most important work was the passing of the **Second Reform Act** which gave the votes to skilled workers by extending the franchise in the boroughs to all householders and to lodgers who paid £10 per annum in rent. Though this was in accord with the political beliefs of Disraeli, it was an act of political astuteness since the workers were clamouring for the vote and there seemed to be an obvious reward for whoever gave it to them. Yet Disraeli's political opportunism failed, because having been given the vote they used it to bring Gladstone into office (1868).

Disraeli's first term as Prime Minister came with Lord Derby's resignation in 1868. It was a poor reward for Disraeli's very patient wait, since he had no majority and no chance of putting his ideas into practice. Gladstone, who had just taken over from Lord John Russell as leader of the new Liberal Party, forced a general election on the question of the disestablishment of the Anglican Church in Ireland. A Liberal majority of 112 seats gave Gladstone the office of Prime Minister.

Gladstone's first ministry (1868–74)

His early career fitted him for the premiership. He was the son of a Liverpool merchant and was educated at Eton and Oxford. He entered the House of Commons as the Conservative member for Newark. His first government post came in Peel's '100 Days'. In Peel's second ministry, he became President of the Board of Trade and a convert to free trade. After Peel's fall, he became leader of the Peelites. In 1852, he became Chancellor of the Exchequer under Aberdeen and brought in a free trade budget. In Palmerston's second ministry, he brought in a further free trade budget and the Cobden Treaty (1860). On the death of Palmerston, Gladstone came out in favour of parliamentary reform and although his bill, in 1866, failed, he succeeded Russell to the leadership in 1868.

First ministry—Irish affairs were his special concern and he duly brought in the following reforms:

1. **The Irish church** was disestablished and disendowed. In this way, the Roman Catholic majority no longer had to pay tithes to the alien Anglican Church, whilst the endowments

were partially confiscated and used for secular purposes (1869).

2. **The Irish Land Act** restricted the power of the Irish landlord. Tenants who paid their rent were not to be evicted and compensation was to be paid for improvements. Government loans were made available for tenants who wished to buy. The act failed in that it did not prevent landlords from raising the rent and then evicting for non-payment (1870).

3. **The Irish University Bill** tried to set up higher education for Catholics but it failed to pass the House of Commons (1873). Of Gladstone's Irish enactments, only the first was a success, he returned to the Irish question in later ministries.

Domestic affairs also were the subject of much legislation:

1. **Forster's Elementary Education Act** (1870) laid the foundations of our national system of education. It was made necessary by the 1867 Reform Act ('We must educate our masters'—Robert Lowe). It divided England into districts and where no school existed, it set up a state elementary school under a local School Board. It laid down that religious education in these schools must be nonsectarian. Board schools and voluntary schools were both to get a government grant but the latter were not entitled to a local rate and had to depend on their endowments.

2. **The University Test Act** (1871) abolished the religious test of participating in Holy Communion for entry and scholarships to Oxford and Cambridge universities. (The government remained outside the drive for Grammar School and University education for girls, preferring to leave it to the Misses Buss, Beale and Davies).

3. **Cardwell's Army Reforms** (1871) were long overdue:
The Secretary for War was to be supreme and was to have an Army Council to assist him with the C. in C. no longer independent. The army was to consist of volunteers and to number 500 000. The period of enlistment was reduced from 20 to 12 years, of which, 6 years was to be on active service and 6 in the reserve. County regiments were to have linked battalions (one at home and one on active service). Commonwealth establishments were cut. The sale of commissions was abolished to get better officers. Annual manoeuvres and breach loading rifles were introduced to improve efficiency and flogging was abolished in peace time.

4. **Civil Service Reforms** (1871) introduced the idea of recruiting to the Home civil service by means of open competitive exams. The Civil Service Commission was to conduct these examinations.

5. **Trade Unions** were given legal recognition, which enabled them to own property and use the courts to sue absconding officials by the Trade Unions Act (1871), but lost the right to picket even peacefully, by the Criminal Law Amendment Act, later the same year.

6. **The Ballot Act** (1872) attempted to get rid of bribery and intimidation at elections by establishing the secret ballot which replaced the open hustings by the ballot box.

7. **The Licensing Act** (1872), in response to pressure from Bruce and the United Kingdom Alliance, closed public houses where they were over-plentiful, limited opening hours and regulated against the adulteration of drink.

8. **Rigid Economy** was practised in finance and income tax was reduced from 7 pence to 3 pence in the £.

Foreign affairs were not Gladstone's forte and his handling of them received a good deal of criticism:

The most important event that Gladstone and Granville had to deal with was the **Franco-Prussian War** (1870–71). Britain's army was small by continental standards and Gladstone was content to make sure that Belgian neutrality was respected. Bismarck's recent publication in 'The Times' of French designs on Belgium had made public opinion in this country turn against France.

When Russia announced that she would no longer be bound by the **Black Sea clause** of the Treaty of Paris, Britain was able to save face by agreeing to the change at a conference in London (1871). Gladstone was greatly criticized, when, in 1872, he agreed to submit the '**Alabama**' claim to arbitration. At the time, this seemed a weakness to many. However, even though the five judges awarded the U.S.A. £3¼ million damages, the settlement did end the bad feeling between the two countries and they have remained on good terms ever since.

The election of 1874 was the first to be held under the terms of the Ballot Act and Gladstone hoped for success on a plan to end income tax. However, the government was a spent force, likened by Disraeli to 'a range of exhausted volcanoes'. Moreover, each of Gladstone's reforms had upset some group of electors (e.g. the brewers were particularly upset by the Licensing Act). In the event, the electorate gave Disraeli his first and only period of office with a majority.

Disraeli's second ministry

At last Disraeli could put his ideas into practice. His main interest at this time was foreign (including imperial) affairs.

However, he did not forget his old radical tendencies and his Home Secretary, Richard Cross, was kept busy introducing a list of reforms which greatly extended the size and scope of government activity. This might be regarded by some as the first step towards a collectivist state.

Social reforms were surprisingly frequent for a Conservative ministry and reflect Disraeli's continuing interest in an alliance with the working classes.

The Factory Act of 1874 introduced the 56 hour week. With 6 of these coming on Saturday, the 10 hour day may be said to have now been achieved.

The Public Health Act of 1875 consolidated previous acts such as the act of 1848, which may be regarded as the basis of all such laws, and required local authorities to appoint medical officers of health and sanitary inspectors. It also gave these authorities wide powers over water supply, sewage disposal and infectious diseases.

The act was accompanied by a River Pollution Act and a Sale of Food and Drugs Act, which show that there was concern over the environment then.

The Artisans' Dwellings Act empowered local authorities to condemn slums and erect better houses in their place. The act was applied with especial vigour in Birmingham where Joseph Chamberlain was making a name for himself as mayor (1875).

The Enclosure of Commons Act was an attempt to check enclosure for agricultural purposes, except where it was in the public interest. This act made it possible to preserve open spaces near cities for public use. An example of this is the preservation of Epping Forest (1875).

The Climbing Boys' Act (1875) at last made effective the ban on the use of young boys as sweeps, by requiring their masters to take out an annual licence.

The Conspiracy & Protection of Property Act (1875) pleased trades unions by legalizing picketing so long as it was peaceful. This made it possible, once again, to entertain the idea of a strike.

The Employers' and Workmen's Act (1875) made breach of contract on the part of an employee a civil instead of a criminal offence. This put him on a par with the employer, for whom it was already a civil offence.

An Education Act (1876) tried to make school attendance compulsory but children and their parents combined to defeat it until education was made free as well as compulsory in 1891.

The Merchant Shipping Act (1876) was delayed in the

House, to the anger of Plimsoll, who alleged that ship owners allowed ships to leave port overloaded. Thus they would either gain large profits or the insurance if the ship should be sunk. The government took up Plimsoll's private members bill and made it a legal requirement to have a loading mark on ships. Unfortunately it was left to the owners to fix where the line should go.

A Factory and Workshops Act (1878) consolidated 45 acts into one. It prohibited all employment of children under ten, although many small workshops managed to ignore the law because of the difficulty of enforcing it in small workshops.

Following the failure of the Glasgow City Bank, many shareholders were ruined and the government sought to avoid any repetition of this by the **Limited Liability Act** (1879), which limited the liability of shareholders to the amount of their share.

Foreign and imperial policy

Disraeli himself took a very keen interest in foreign policy; he believed that it should be directed towards building up the fame of the country and the prestige of the monarch.

The Purchase of the Suez Canal Shares (1875) was a real coup on the part of Disraeli. The canal had been built with Egyptian labour and French capital by the French engineer Ferdinand de Lesseps. It was opened with the Khedive owning 40% of the shares (1869). Disraeli heard that the Khedive, a spendthrift, was willing to sell his shares. Borrowing the money from the Rothschilds, he paid £4 000 000 for 40% of the shares and thus made Britain the largest single shareholder of a waterway that was vital to our shipping.

The Prince of Wales chafed under the inaction forced upon him by the Queen and Disraeli sent him on a mission to India which was to prove very successful. It led to the offer of the title of **Empress of India** to the Queen in 1876. This seemed to put her on a par with the monarchs of Austria, Russia and Germany and it certainly pleased Queen Victoria who returned the favour by the elevation of Disraeli to the peerage as the first Earl of Beaconsfield.

In South Africa, Disraeli's forward policy led Britain into a war. Sir Theophilus Shepstone was sent to the Transvaal when the Boers felt threatened by the Zulus. The Boers were very short of funds and in no condition to face Cetewayo. They were willing to come into the British Empire in return for protection and so the Transvaal was annexed (1877). Two year's later there followed the Zulu War, where Britain suffered the defeat of a column at Isandhlwana before Cetewayo was captured at Ulundi and the Zulus crushed.

In Afghanistan, too, there was war. Lord Lytton, the Viceroy sent an army to depose the pro-Russian amir (1878) and to install a new one. This led to a rising (The Second Afghan War) against the British. Finally Kandahar had to be relieved by Lord Roberts in his famous cross-country march from Kabul. This saved the army but led to the reversal of the forward policy by Gladstone.

The Eastern Question was re-opened in 1875, when the Turks were faced with a rising of their Christian subjects in the Balkans. In Bulgaria, the rising was put down by Turkish irregulars with appalling cruelty. This gave Russia the excuse to attack Turkey ostensibly to protect the Christians. Gladstone gave a lead in Britain to the protest against the atrocities of the Turks and demanded that they should be cleared out 'bag and baggage' from the province. Disraeli was in no mood to intervene, preferring to play down the atrocities until the fall of Plevna after an heroic defence, when British public opinion turned in favour of the Turks. Amidst a display of jingoism by the queen and her subjects, £6 000 000 was voted by parliament for military purposes, the Mediterranean Fleet was moved up through the Straits and both Britain and Austria demanded a European conference, when Russia's terms to Turkey, in the **Treaty of San Stefano** (1878) were known.

The Congress of Berlin, called by Bismarck, to avoid war between his two allies, was dominated by Disraeli. Armed with preliminary agreements with Russia, Austria and Turkey, he was able to insist on a revision of the treaty, which trisected the proposed Russian puppet state of Bulgaria, gave the administration of Bosnia and Herzegovina to Austria, ceded Cyprus to Britain.

Disraeli claimed to have brought back 'Peace with honour' from the Congress, although doubts were expressed by Lord Salisbury who said that 'we backed the wrong horse'.

Disraeli's defeat at the polls in 1880 and his death in 1881, left Gladstone to dominate the next decade.

Gladstone Supreme

Gladstone's second ministry

At home the period 1880–85, saw the impending break in the Liberal Party. It was an ill-assorted cabinet, reflecting a wide range of opinion within the party. It was held together by the personal eloquence and popularity of Gladstone and owed its success at the polls to the organization of Chamberlain. Chamberlain's programme of manhood suffrage, free education, the payment of M.Ps. and special taxes on the rich got no support from the Whigs and little enthusiasm from Gladstone himself.

Parliamentary Reform must be its greatest achievement:
1. **The Corrupt Practices Act** (1883) was a determined attempt to stop bribery and corruption at elections. It sought to define and limit election expenses.
2. **The Reform Act** (1884) gave the vote to rural householders including farm labourers, adding 2 000 000 voters to the list.
3. **The Redistribution Act** (1885) represented an approach to the idea of single member constituencies. Towns with less than 15 000 inhabitants lost their separate representation in parliament; towns with a population between 15 000 and 50 000 had one member; large towns such as London, and counties were divided up into a number of single member constituencies.
The Bradlaugh Case wasted a considerable amount of parliament's time. This radical M.P., who was an atheist and refused to take the oath was the centre of dispute throughout the ministry and was not allowed to take his seat until 1886.
In Ireland Gladstone tried hard to solve Ireland's problems but met with little success:
1. **W.E. Forster**, Chief Secretary tried to end crime with the help of the Coercion Act (1880), so that a Second Land Act could be introduced.
2. **The Second Land Act** (1881) gave the Irish tenants Fair rents, Fixity of tenure and Free sale. Parnell's Land League would not co-operate; they set their own rents and evictions and outrages continued. Irish leaders, including Parnell, were arrested and kept in Kilmainham Gaol, Dublin.
3. Gladstone made an agreement with Parnell, known as the **Kilmainham Treaty**, by which Parnell would end crime in Ireland and the government would cancel arrears of rent (1882).

4. **The Phoenix Park Murders** (1882) ruined any chance of success that the Kilmainham Treaty might have had. The new Chief Secretary for Ireland, Lord Frederick Cavendish, who replaced W.E. Forster as a token of the government's intention of ending its policy of coercion, and his Under-Secretary, Burke, were set upon by a gang of extremists calling themselves 'The Invincibles' and stabbed to death.
5. Parnell was blamed for the murder and there was a return to coercion by the **Crimes Act** (1883).

Imperial & foreign affairs went badly for the government:
1. In **South Africa**, the Boers expected Gladstone to restore their independence because he had so strongly criticized Disraeli's act of annexation. Gladstone delayed while the Boers acted. They defeated a British force at Majuba Hill and claimed their right to independence. Gladstone, refused to use arms to keep them in the Empire and agreed to the **convention of Pretoria** (1881), when Boer independence was recognized.
2. **Bechuanaland** and **Matabeleland** were annexed in an unusual burst of imperialism (1885).
3. Gladstone's agreement to the German annexation of Northern **New Guinea** and **Samoa** was resented in New Zealand and Australia.
4. The unpopularity of Gladstone's foreign policy was temporarily checked when he prepared to maintain the independence of **Afghanistan** against Russia (1885).
5. Events in Egypt and the Sudan finally led to the downfall of Gladstone's government:

In **Egypt**, resentment against the interference in their country by Britain and France (Dual Control), led to a revolt against the foreigner under **Arabi Pasha** (1881). France withdrew from the proposed punitive expedition and Britain acted alone. The navy bombarded Alexandria and the army, under Sir Garnet Wolseley, after a forced march, defeated Arabi's forces at Tel-el-Kebir. Gladstone might well have annexed Egypt, since the British army was the only effective force there, but he chose instead merely to occupy the country and to send **Sir Evelyn Baring** (later Lord Cromer) to administer it. Meanwhile, the **Sudan** was being overrun by the forces of the **Mahdi** and an Anglo-Egyptian force under General Hicks was defeated. Gladstone had to decide whether to abandon the Sudan or to send a new force against the Mahdi. It was decided to send troops to evacuate all the Sudan, South of Wadi Halfa. The command was given to **General Gordon** who decided to make a stand at Khartoum.

Gladstone felt that Gordon should have referred such a decision to higher authority. He had not wished to get involved in the Southern Sudan and he delayed taking action. When in January 1885, a relieving force did reach Khartoum, it was to find that it had been stormed and Gordon killed two days before. The news of the **death of Gordon** brought down the government, over a vote on the budget.

Salisbury's caretaker government

Lord Salisbury, with no majority, could only form a ministry pending a general election. The ministry lasted seven months, during which time only two events of importance took place: **Burma** had been reduced to an inland state with Britain administering Lower Burma. King Thibaw, expecting French help, confiscated property belonging to the Bombay-Burma Company. After an ultimatum, Upper Burma was invaded, Thibaw deposed and his country annexed (January 1886).

Irish support had enabled Lord Salisbury to form a ministry and he was anxious to retain that support. Firm government was to be tempered by concessions and Lord Ashbourne's Act was passed which made state loans available to the Irish peasants who wished to buy their land.

A tentative approach was also made to Parnell with a view to giving the **Irish Home Rule** in exchange for their support, in elections, in towns such as Liverpool and Glasgow where the Irish vote was strong. Since Gladstone, unwilling to appear to be bidding for the Irish vote, did not reply to Parnell's advances, Parnell ordered the Irish to vote Conservative at the General Election of 1885.

Chamberlain, hoping for a Liberal victory, revealed his famous 'unauthorized programme' of social reform, which won the vote of the country constituencies, where farm labourers had received the vote in Gladstone's second ministry.

The result of the election was a majority of 86 for Liberals over Conservatives, with the Irish also having 86 seats and thus having the power to decide which party should be in office. When Gladstone's son let it be known that his father had been converted to the need for Home Rule for Ireland, Lord Salisbury dropped his plans and Parnell used the Irish vote in the Commons to defeat the Government and so bring Gladstone back to office for the third time. Gladstone, however, had the problem of explaining his sudden conversion to Home Rule and the further task of carrying his party with him.

Gladstone's third ministry

Gladstone was now dependent upon the Irish vote for his majority and he was virtually committed to introducing Home Rule, although not all of his cabinet or his party were in favour of such an action. Furthermore the English people had become convinced by 'troubles' in Ireland that the Irish were not fit to govern themselves. Dynamite outrages in London seemed only to confirm this view.

The Home Rule Bill (1886) proposed to set up an Irish Parliament in Dublin. There should also be an executive which administered the legislation on all but important, reserved subjects: these were matters affecting the Crown, war and peace, defence, foreign affairs and overseas trade. No Irish members were to sit at Westminster but there was to be a right of appeal from Irish courts to the judicial committee of the Privy Council. Gladstone was never able to win over key men in his own party, such as Lord Hartington, leader of the Whigs and Joseph Chamberlain, a cabinet minister and leader of the Radicals. As a result, 93 Liberals voted with the Conservatives and the Bill was rejected in the Commons by 343 to 313 (the largest vote on record in the House).

Gladstone resigned and appealed to the country. The people now showed how much they were against Home Rule. Gladstone mustered only 191 Liberals and 85 Irish seats to the 316 Conservatives and 78 Liberals who were opposed to Home Rule. Salisbury came into power with a majority of 118; the Liberals were split and stayed out of office for twenty years (with one short break); Home Rule ceased to be a real issue until the time of the Parliament Act.

Gladstone's fourth ministry

Concerned as it was with the Second Home Rule Bill, Gladstone's fourth ministry might best be considered here as a kind of addendum to his third ministry.

The second Home Rule Bill (1893) was Gladstone's main consideration when he took office. However, although he had a majority of 40, he was dependent upon the Irish vote and at the age of 83, he only kept going by his determination to finish his Irish plan. The bill was similar to the previous one except that it allowed for Irish representation at Westminster. It was keenly contested at all stages but eventually passed the Commons with a majority of 34, but was rejected in the Lords on the grounds that the British people were against it. Gladstone should have gone to the country but allowed himself to be persuaded to remain in power. This enabled him to pass the Local Government Act.

The Local Government Act (1894) is more generally known as the Parish Councils Bill. Its passage was strongly contested in both houses before it became law. By it:

1. 6 880 parish councils were set up. On paper they had wide powers, but their lack of funds caused their powers to be little used.

2. It completed the framework of local government by dividing the counties into urban and rural districts. Each district had its own democratically elected council and allowed both single and married women to vote and to be elected to the council. This was a major step towards the emancipation of women.

The Employers' Liability Bill (1894) was mutilated in the Lords by the addition of a contracting out clause. The increased use of the veto by the Lords did not go unnoticed by Gladstone who foresaw that this would become an issue between the two houses.

Gladstone resigned in March 1894 with a long record of public service behind him; the queen, of her own wish, sent for Lord Rosebery to replace him.

Rosebery's ministry

Lord Rosebery was not chosen by Gladstone nor by the Liberal Party but by the queen. He was not fitted to hold the party together. He was not on speaking terms with Sir William Harcourt, who led the party in the Commons and was regarded by many as the natural successor to Gladstone. He remained in office for nearly 16 months and had most of his legislation vetoed by the House of Lords. Thus the radical '**Newcastle Programme**', formally adopted by the party in 1891, which included such measures as Home Rule, Disestablishment in Wales and Scotland, local right of veto on the sale of intoxicating liquor and the abolition of the plural vote, came to nothing. Thus the impending struggle between the two houses was brought nearer.

Harcourt's budget (1894), did escape the veto. It included a system of progressive death duties which has been with us ever since. Other measures were a penny on income tax, sixpence on a barrel of beer and sixpence on a gallon of spirits. Finally the government resigned over a snap vote of censure as to the amount of cordite the army should use.

Lord Salisbury as Prime Minister

Although Lord Salisbury is famous for his opposition to the 2nd Reform Act (1867) which he called, 'A leap in the dark', his main interest was in foreign affairs. His dictum that, 'We backed the wrong horse' at the Congress of Berlin has been widely quoted and he gave his name to the capital of Rhodesia.

Salisbury's second ministry (1886–92)

Gladstone's Home Rule Bill had given Salisbury office with power and a weakened opposition. He took a personal interest in foreign affairs while **Lord Randolph Churchill** at the age of only 37, became the Chancellor of the Exchequer and Leader of the Commons; his Dartford speech outlined a great programme of reforms while in the Balkans he envisaged Britain leading the Balkan peoples to their independence. This was the high water mark of his career; before the end of the year he had resigned over his budget and was succeeded as Chancellor by G.J. Goschen.

In home affairs Salisbury believed in practical details rather than principles. Perhaps the most important piece of legislation was the **Local Government Act** of 1888. This continued the process, started in 1835, of making local government more democratic. The act established 62 county councils and a number of county boroughs. In both cases the council was elected by the ratepayers who had already been enfranchised by the 3rd Reform Act. In this case women ratepayers were allowed to vote as long as they were single. These new authorities took over much of the work of the J.P. London's size ensured that it was treated as a separate problem by the **London County Council Act**. The various vestries and district boards were now replaced by a single council which had authority over the whole area except the historic City of London. These County Councils were to be subdivided by the act of 1894.

Free elementary education was established by an act of 1891 and this made it at last possible to insist that it should be also compulsory in fact as well as in name.

A Factory Act of 1891 raised the minimum age for employing children in factories to 11: it also fixed the maximum working hours per day for women at 12 and set $1\frac{1}{2}$ hours for meals.

A Tithes Act of 1891 made tithes payable by the owner of the land and not by the occupier. This ended, for many years, the tenant's fear that cattle or movables might be distrained for non-payment of tithe.

The Small Holdings Act of 1892 empowered County Councils to form agricultural small holdings by borrowing. It proved to be a dead letter.

Possibly the most important domestic event of this ministry was the **London Dock Strike** (1889). This came at a time when the public were becoming more aware of the poverty that existed and trade unions were becoming more militant, ready to strike to improve their lot rather than as a protest against falling standards. The successful strike for the 'dockers' tanner' triggered off a rapid growth in trade union membership. Its significance was that this had been the first successful attempt to show what unskilled men could do if properly led.

In Ireland, Salisbury's nephew, Balfour emerged as a strong man, earning for himself the title of 'Bloody Balfour'. His efforts for firm rule were begun by a **Crimes Act** (1887) to enable the government to deal with the Irish 'Plan of Campaign', but they were also accompanied by an attempt to win over the Irish away from Home Rule. To this end, a new **Land Act** (1887) extended Gladstone's act of 1881 and a new **Land Purchase Act** (1890) set up a central office to deal with all land problems in Ireland. Relief works in poverty-stricken and congested areas were also begun.

Parnell reached the peak of his influence when a series of letters in 'The Times', under the heading '**Parnellism and Crime**' were proved to be the work of Pigott, a poor journalist, who later confessed to the forgery. The failure of this attempt to implicate Parnell in the Phoenix Park murders raised his stock with the British public.

Yet within twelve months, his involvement in the **O'Shea divorce**, lost him the support of the Irish catholics and any chance he had of leading Ireland to independence.

Foreign policy became Lord Salisbury's personal concern when he took over the foreign office in 1887. In this year, the Queen's Golden Jubilee sparked off a wave of patriotism which had its main political effect in a surge of imperialism. The presence of the Prime Ministers of the self governing colonies, for the jubilee, made it possible for them to consult with the home government in a **Colonial Conference** which turned out to be the first of many. In this ministry, Salisbury carried out a bold and aggressive imperial policy. Encouraging chartered companies to open up and occupy territory, the government secured their gains by the conclusion of treaties with those powers who had adjoining areas of influence. In this way Britain was able to play a considerable part in the 'Scramble for Africa':

In West Africa, the Royal Niger Company (founded 1886) developed trade in the region of the Lower Niger, to forestall the French. This area came under the Crown in 1900.

In East Africa, the British East Africa Company (founded 1888) safeguarded Kenya and Uganda. By a treaty with Germany (1890) Zanzibar was gained in exchange for Heligoland and the boundaries of neighbouring colonies in East Africa settled. There followed similar treaties with France and the Congo Free State (1890) and with Italy, partitioning Somaliland in 1891.

In South Africa, Salisbury's government, in support of the British South Africa Company, furthered Rhodes' dream of a Cape to Cairo railway by taking over Bechuanaland (1885) and Matabeleland (1888). A treaty with Portugal (1890) defined the boundary with Angola and denied Portugal's claim to the hinterland between the two Portuguese territories of Angola and Mozambique.

In Egypt, Salisbury found himself unable to end the British occupation and indeed Lord Cromer was busily and with the utmost of economy, carrying out a programme of 'water and justice'. Far from leaving Egypt, Salisbury's next government was to see the reconquest of the Sudan.

In the Far East, another scramble for territory occurred, with Britain annexing over one hundred islands in the Pacific Ocean, placing many under the control of New Zealand.

Salisbury's third ministry

In this ministry, Salisbury, uniting Conservatives and Liberal-Unionists had a majority of 152 over Liberal and Irish. Again, Salisbury combined the foreign office with his position of Prime Minister, with the inevitable emphasis on foreign affairs. The strongest and most popular minister proved to be a Liberal-Unionist, Joseph Chamberlain, who, though only Colonial Secretary, had to be treated with respect by Salisbury and Balfour

In home affairs the government was prepared to follow Chamberlain's lead into social reform, but since he was now pre-occupied with imperial matters, not much was done.

The one important measure was the **Workmen's Compensation Act** (1897) which laid down that employers were responsible for accidents to workmen during the course of their employment. This was extended in 1907 to cover other categories of workers such as seamen, who especially needed it. In 1896, a **Committee on Old Age Pensions** with Lord Rothschild as chairman, examined over 100 schemes, but did not recommend any. A subsequent select committee recommended five shillings a week to deserving poor, over 65, but the expense of the Boer War ended the plan.

An **Agricultural Rates Bill** (1896), remitted one half of farm rates and thus was the first example of derating.

The **Khaki Election** (1900) found the Liberals split over the issue of Imperialism: they suffered a heavy defeat. The election made little difference to the situation in the Commons, but what was important was the foundation (1900) of the **Labour Representation Committee,** with Ramsay McDonald as secretary. They aimed at increasing the number of Labour M.P.s. in the Commons and the trade unions agreed to raise a levy to support them. This was the beginning of the Labour Party.

In Ireland the government returned to their former policy of 'firmness and kindness'.

A Land Purchase Act of 1896 was followed by the more sweeping **Wyndham's Act** of 1903. Wyndham, a disciple of Balfour, brought in an act where a cash contribution by the state bridged the gap between what the tenant could pay and what the landlord was asking.

Elected County Councils were set up (1898).

Sir Horace Plunkett established the Irish Agricultural Society to stimulate the formation of **co-operatives**.

Land Purchase legislation and co-operatives had the desired effect of bringing prosperity to Ireland in the shape of self respecting small farmers. Nevertheless, the Irish were not won over from the desire for Home Rule. Even the policy of encouraging a sense of nationalism, divorced from Home Rule, through the language and literature was not a success.

Imperial and foreign affairs received a stimulus from Queen Victoria's Diamond Jubilee (1897). The popular enthusiasm that it generated coincided with the enthusiasm of **Joseph Chamberlain** at the Colonial office, for his new scheme for developing the Empire scientifically, as a unit similar to Germany's Zollverein. This, coupled with tariffs on foreign goods would enable Britain to compete successfully with her new trade rivals. The Colonial Conference at the time of the Jubilee, gave Chamberlain a golden opportunity to spread propaganda for his scheme. It was resolved that the Colonial Conferences should be held at intervals.

This policy did involve a risk of war which was narrowly averted over Venezuela but not averted in the Sudan or in Rhodesia. War with France was narrowly averted after Fashoda.

The Boundary Dispute between **Britain and Venezuela** over the border with British Guiana, was not attributable to any 'forward' policy on the part of Britain. President Cleveland intervened to declare that the boundary would be drawn up by an American commission. His revival of the Monroe Doctrine was electioneering and the matter was settled reasonably by diplomacy but it did serve to highlight Britain's isolation in a Europe falling into two camps (1896).

In 1896, the government began the slow reconquest of the **Sudan**. Britain had not given up her position in Egypt and felt that the continued presence of the Mahdi in the Sudan was a threat to the security of Egypt. Accordingly **Kitchener** began the campaign, which involved the building of a railway to supply his forces. With the aid of the maxim gun, the fanatical dervishes were defeated at **Atbara** and at **Omdurman**. While completing the occupation, Kitchener's forces came face to face with French forces under Major Marchand who had marched 2 800 miles from West Africa and who were claiming the Sudan. Sensibly, the two commanders referred the matter to their governments and the French, unwillingly, ordered their forces to withdraw from **Fashoda**. Britain and Egypt set up a joint government over the Sudan, where subsequently reforms similar to those of Cromer in Egypt, were carried out under Wingate.

In India, Lord Curzon as Viceroy (1899–1905), carried out a policy of reforms in all departments—a police force, irrigation schemes and peasant co-operatives. A more aggressive frontier policy was also followed.

The Second Boer War (1899–1902), though partly the result of a long history of antagonism between Boer and Briton in South Africa, was undoubtedly hastened by the British occupation of Rhodesia. The Uitlander problem became the excuse for the Jameson Raid which Rhodes encouraged, seeing it as promising the Cape to Cairo Railway he had dreamed about. Emboldened by German aid, Kruger rejected moderate counsels and seemed to welcome the war.

After initial Boer success, when British forces were beseiged in Ladysmith, Kimberley and Mafeking, Kitchener and Roberts, supplied with reinforcements, were able to defeat the Boers. However, the final stage, with its guerilla warfare and concentration camps, caused Campbell Bannerman to speak of 'methods of barbarism' on the part of the British.

The Treaty of Vereeniging (1902) refrained from punishing civilians who had borne arms, promised the Boers self government in the British Empire and granted £3 000 000 to the Boer farmers to restock their farms.

The promise of self government was fulfilled in 1906 and in 1910 the two British colonies, Cape Colony and Natal were joined with the two Boer states, Transvaal and the Orange Free State to form the **Union of South Africa**. The old Boer attitude towards the natives remained and produced the policy of 'Apartheid' which causes so many problems for South Africa today.

Salisbury's foreign policy was to avoid committing Britain to any firm alliance thus leaving her free to decide each course of action on its merits. This policy of **'Splendid Isolation'** left the country dangerously isolated in a world of great alliances. The rejection of Chamberlain's offer of an alliance by Germany in 1898 and Britain's obvious isolation during the Boer War made it imperative for Britain to look for allies in view of Germany's coolness and the drive to colonial expansion on the part of France and Russia, now united in a Dual Alliance at odds with the Triple Alliance of Germany, Austria and Italy.

The Anglo-Japanese Alliance (1902) marks Britain's first step out of isolation and left Japan free to face up to Russian expansion in Manchuria and Korea, secure in the knowledge that if another European power supported Russia, Britain would come to the aid of Japan. It also left Britain secure in the knowledge of Japanese help in the Pacific in the event of a war in Europe.

Balfour's ministry

Salisbury's nephew, Arthur Balfour became Prime Minister when his uncle retired in 1902. He did not achieve any great volume of reforms nor did he make any important change in the direction of Conservative policy in Ireland. Perhaps his most notable achievement was the conclusion of the **Entente Cordiale** with France.

At home the **Education Act** (1902) made important changes:

1. County Councils took over the administration of elementary education from the School Boards and became responsible for the running costs of church schools, leaving them to find the money for the upkeep of the school fabric.

2. County Councils established secondary schools which pro-

vided a ladder in education whereby a poor boy could proceed by means of scholarships from the elementary to the secondary school and thence to university.

Sectarian jealousy again raised its head when the Nonconformists protested at the increased aid, from the rates, for the church schools.

Joseph Chamberlain resigned from the post of Colonial Secretary in 1903, to campaign for his scheme for tariff reform, which would mean the end of free trade. This scheme was not popular with some of the party, led by the Duke of Devonshire. Balfour sat feebly on the fence, allowing the division in the party to develop into a major split and allowing the government to lose a succession of by-elections and a number of able men who crossed over to the Liberals.

The Licensing Act of 1904 took the view that brewery shareholders had rights but that they must give way to the public good. So the act established the principle that where public houses were closed, not for misconduct but for the good of the public, then, compensation should be paid to the shareholders from a fund to be levied from the trade.

In Ireland Wyndham's Land Act finally ended the land problem by lending tenants £5 000 000 per annum at $3\frac{1}{2}\%$ to buy their farms. A quarter of a million tenants took advantage of the scheme in six years.

However the demand for Home Rule remained.

In foreign affairs there was one notable achievement. Lord Landsdowne and Edward VII established good relations with France. Visits were exchanged and the differences between the two countries explored. By the **Entente Cordiale** (1904), minor colonial disputes were settled and Britain recognized France's special position in Morocco in exchange for French recognition of the British position in Egypt and the Sudan. The importance of the entente may be gauged by Germany's swift move to test its strength.

Chinese Labour in South Africa brought protests from Australia and New Zealand and even more from the working classes whose hopes that labour should no longer be treated as a mere commodity received a setback.

The general election (1906)

On the resignation of Balfour in 1905, Campbell-Bannerman took office and prepared for a general election. This was fought on a number of issues:

1. **Free trade** was the major concern. The Liberals looked

upon it as the foundation of our national prosperity and raised the bogey of dear bread by their poster showing a Tory small loaf and a Liberal large loaf. The Tory Party was still deeply divided on this issue with Chamberlain vociferous for protection.

2. **Imperialism** had become discredited with the electorate because of the excesses of the Boer War and the issues raised by 'Chinese Slavery' in South Africa. The leading Liberals had condemned the war whilst the Tories were identified with Imperialism.

3. **The Nonconformists** were bitter over the Tory Education Act of 1902 and turned to the Liberals to introduce further legislation to redress their grievances.

4. **In Ireland** the Tory recipe of '20 years firm rule' had failed to kill the demand for Home Rule and the Liberals were prepared to introduce another Home Rule Bill in exchange for Irish votes.

5. The Liberals, unlike the Tories, were in favour of a policy of **social reform** and the nation felt that this was now overdue.

6. **The trade unions** were demanding legislation to reverse the Taff Vale Judgement and the Liberals were prepared to do this.

7. The Tories were blamed for the **lack of national prosperity**.

8. **The swing of the pendulum**, more regular before the war, meant that the voters were ready to give the Liberals a turn in office.

The result was a massive Liberal victory with the Liberals gaining 377 seats and the combined opposition only 293. Conservative gaining 157, Irish 83, Labour 53. The stage appeared to be set for a massive programme of Liberal reforms. However, two considerations required thought:

1. The Conservatives were prepared to use their majority in the **House of Lords** to thwart Liberal measures to such an extent that they precipitated a constitutional crisis by opposing the budget and thereby bringing up the question of reforming the second chamber.

2. The Liberals were divided in their attitude to **Imperialism** with some like Lloyd George and Morley following the Prime Minister's lead and others like Rosebery, Asquith, Grey and Haldane taking a pro-Imperialist view. This was to show when it came to issues like 'Chinese Slavery'.

Liberal Government

The Liberal Government (1906) attained the high water mark of Liberal achievement in this country, in which it laid the foundations of the Welfare State and established the supremacy of the House of Commons over the House of Lords. It also saw the start of the Liberal decline which was compounded by the special powers it took to wage war more efficiently. In doing this it introduced many new governmental powers which were the opposite of liberal thinking.

Liberal reforms

In spite of the opposition of the House of Lords, which will be dealt with later, many important reforms were introduced:

The Workmen's Compensation Act (1906) extended the protection given by the act of 1897 to all trades, for injury during the course of employment. There was no need to prove negligence on the part of the employer.

The Trades Disputes Act (1906) reversed the decision of the Taff Vale Judgement, which had stated that trades unions could be sued for damages caused during a strike. This had made it virtually impossible to use the strike weapon. The act restored the legal position that trades unions were not so liable.

The Provision of Meals Act (1906) empowered Local Education Authorities to feed children who came to school hungry. This was an attempt to combat the growing incidence of rickets amongst school children, due to malnutrition.

The Medical Inspection Act (1907) brought elementary school children under medical supervision in the schools.

The Small Holdings Act (1907) gave County Councils powers of compulsory purchase to provide small holdings and allotments.

Army Reforms were the work of R.B. Haldane. The Territorial Army and the O.T.C. were established to prepare a part-time army that could be quickly called to the colours in case of need. This resulted in the rapid mobilization of the B.E.F. in 1914.

The Old Age Pensions Act (1908) established a weekly pension of five shillings per week for a single person and seven shillings and sixpence for a married couple. Recipients had to be British, over 70 years of age and have an income of less than £50 per annum. This was an important defeat for the principle of 'Laissez Faire'.

The Children's Charter (1908) represented an attempt to save young offenders from being brought into contact with hardened criminals so that any chance of reforming their ways was lost. Special courts were set up for these young people where special provisions protected them from evil influences.

The Coal Mines Act (1908) limited the hours of work in the coal mines to eight hours a day.

The Sweated Industries Act (1909) otherwise known as the Trade Boards Act, regulated wages and working conditions in those areas of industry where trade union activity had been ineffective. Boards were set up, consisting of an equal number of representatives of employers and employees, with the task of fixing wages.

The Housing and Town Planning Act (1909) gave Local Authorities the power to demolish insanitary slums and the duty to redevelop the town in an orderly and systematic way.

Labour Exchanges were set up to put employers looking for workmen in touch with workers out of a job. The object was to increase the mobility of labour and to provide information on the availability of jobs in distant parts.

The Osborne Judgement was a ruling by the House of Lords (1909) confirming that it was illegal for a trade union to impose a compulsory levy on its members for political purposes (i.e. to help pay the wages of a Member of Parliament).

The People's Budget (1909) introduced revolutionary taxes to pay for naval armament and social reform. It was rejected by the House of Lords contrary to constitutional custom and the resulting uproar led to the Liberal attempt to reform the House of Lords.

The Parliament Act (1911) was the resulting measure to reform the upper chamber. It laid down that:

The Lords could hold up a money bill (so certified by the Speaker of the Commons) for 28 days only.

They could hold up other bills for two years, after which, if they had been passed three times in two sessions, they could bypass the Lords and go for the royal assent.

Parliament's life was to be changed from seven years to five.

The Payment of M.Ps. was introduced (1911). They received a salary of £400 per annum. This was partly the result of the Osborne Judgement.

The National Insurance Act (1911) was perhaps the most important of these reforms. The act was based upon Bismarck's schemes of 20 years earlier. It was divided into two parts with the first dealing with sickness benefit and the second part dealing with unemployment pay. Both parts of the scheme were compulsory and were financed in part by contributions from the workers by stamps.

The sickness benefit meant free treatment from a doctor, taking part in the scheme and a weekly payment during absence from work. The scheme was administered and the payments made by 'approved' societies (mainly insurance societies and friendly societies).

The unemployment benefit was a weekly payment (dole) to certain classes of workers, when unemployed. Originally this was for not more than fifteen weeks in any one year.

The worker paid 4 pence per week for these benefits, the employer paid 3 pence and the state 2 pence. Lloyd George was able to claim that the workers were getting '9 pence for 4 pence'.

There was considerable opposition, at first, from the medical profession, organized through the British Medical Association, but it gave the average doctor a better income and increased the country's staff of doctors in a short while.

The Shop Hours Act regulated the hours and conditions of shop assistants and provided for a half day's holiday for them by means of an early closing day (1912).

The Third Home Rule Bill was introduced in 1912. Since the elections of 1910, the Liberals had been dependent upon the Irish vote and this was the price to be paid. It was expected to become the first bill to become law under the provisions of the Parliament Act. However, the Unionist Party (Conservatives) encouraged the Ulster protestants to arm themselves and to resist 'Pope rule'. King George V called a conference of interested parties but no progress was made. Finally, the outbreak of the First World War meant that the bill was shelved for the duration.

The Welsh Disestablishment Bill was opposed in the Lords because the Church of England feared that it would be followed by disestablishment in this country. In fact many of the Welsh people were strongly devoted to their chapel and Lloyd George realized the justice of the measure. It had the distinction of being the first bill to become law under the provisions of the Parliament Act.

The Coal Miners Minimum Wages Act (1912) was the first attempt to regulate wages in the mines and based its figures on coal-hewing. It is not possible to say what effect this had on the record output of 287 million tons of coal in 1913, which was never again reached. It marked a departure from 'Laissez Faire'.

The Trade Union Act (1913) reversed the Osborne Judgement whereby the House of Lords, in 1909, had made it illegal for unions to collect a levy from their members to support Labour candidates. The payment of M.Ps. had gone some way to solving the problem and now this act legalized union expenditure for political purposes, provided that such expenditure was approved by a special ballot of the members and that if a member objected to this use of funds, he would have the right to 'contract out', that is he would be allowed to refuse to pay the political levy. This put the onus on the individual.

The struggle with the Lords

The struggle with the House of Lords was of major constitutional importance. It was the final attempt of the Upper House to deny that the Commons as representatives of the nation had the right to the final say in the destinies of the country. **Earlier opposition to the Commons** had been sporadic and had always coincided with those times when a progressive party had a majority in the Lower House:

1. The Reform Bill of 1832 had been rigorously opposed and only forced through by threats to create extra peers.
2. Gladstone's 2nd Home Rule Bill had been rejected on the grounds that the nation was opposed to it. The Lords reserved to themselves the right to interpret the wishes of the nation.
3. Lord Rosebery's attempts to introduce the Newcastle Programme had been rejected by the Lords.

The General Election (1906) gave the Liberals a massive 377 seats so that they considered they had a mandate from the people for a programme of reforms. However, Balfour determined to use his majority in the Lords to prevent the passing of any measure, which, in the judgement of the Lords, did not carry the full support of the nation. Thus many reforms were rejected or so amended as to be unrecognizable:

Education Bill (1906)

Plural Voting Bill (1906)

Two Bills on Land Reform (1906 and 1907)

Small Holdings Bill (1907)

Irish Education Bill (1907)

Licensing Bill (1908).

The People's Budget (1909) may be taken to signify Lloyd George's determination to raise revenue for important social reforms as well as for the naval rearmament, that was now urgent. It may also be regarded as a deliberate attempt to entrap the House of Lords into the unconstitutional step of rejecting the budget, by including a number of revolutionary fiscal measures in the one budget, so as to anger the Lords and make them defy normal usage. It included an increase of 6 pence on the whisky tax and a tax on all licensed premises, which could be seen as an attack upon the brewers: a rise of 2 pence in income tax, a small super tax and a new land tax, which together, could be regarded as class legislation: a tax on motor cars and petrol for the first time as an alternative source of revenue. The budget so incensed the Lords that, in spite of appeals from Edward VII, they took the unprecedented step of rejecting the budget.

This led to a vote of censure in the Commons, dissolution and an **election in January 1910**. This did not give the Liberals the clear cut mandate they sought. The Liberals gained 275 votes, the Conservative-Unionists 273 votes, the Irish 80 votes and the Labour 40. Thus the Irish held the balance in the House and could demand a price for supporting the Liberals (that price was to be Home Rule). Meanwhile the Lords could still cling to the argument that the Liberals did not have overwhelming support in the country.

With the **death of Edward VII** (May 1910), George V called a constitutional conference and the Lords passed the budget, but they were not prepared to compromise on the question of the powers of the House of Lords.

Asquith and the king both hoped that the mere threat to create a large number of Liberal peers to pass the bill would be enough to coerce the Lords. This was not so, at this stage, and the king promised to create some 250 Liberal peers (sufficient to pass a measure reducing the powers of the Lords) on the condition that the Liberals held and won another election.

The election of December 1910 gave the Liberals 272 seats to 272 Conservative-Unionist, but with the support of 84 Irish and 42 Labour, there was a clear majority in support of the Parliament Bill. It was presented to the Lords in May 1911 and the 'Ditchers, who had threatened to fight to the 'last ditch', finally gave in; the bill passed by 131 to 114 votes and Balfour resigned in favour of Bonar Law.

The Parliament Act defined the terms of the Lords veto (page 48) but in so doing, appeared to strengthen the Lords. They could now hold up money bills for 28 days and other bills for two years and it appeared that they were prepared to use this power frequently. The act was amended by the Labour government in 1949 to limit the period of delay to one year.

The suffragettes

John Stuart Mill advocated votes for women in his writings and speeches: he even obtained 73 votes in favour of his amendment to this effect, to Disraeli's Reform Bill in 1867. However, the majority of Victorians agreed with their queen when she said that 'We women are not made for governing'. This was beginning to change and by 1900, Mrs Millicent Fawcett was leading the cause of women's suffrage in a constitutional way. In 1903 Mrs Pankhurst founded the **Women's Social and Political Union** to press for Women's suffrage by any means, legal or illegal. With the help of her daughters, Christabel and Sylvia, and Mrs Pethick-Lawrence the movement became militant. Women chained themselves to railings, slashed pictures in the National Gallery, heckled speakers, set fire to houses and pillar boxes and one even threw herself in front of the King's horse in the Derby. When imprisoned, they went on hunger strike.

The Cat and Mouse Act (1913) allowed the authorities to release hunger-strikers, only to return them to prison without further trial, if they were again arrested.

The war gave women an opportunity to show what they could do and in 1918, the long-delayed right to vote was given to women over 30, while the following year, Lady Astor became the first woman member of parliament.

Trade unions

The start of the twentieth century saw militancy in the trade union movement. This was a period when prices rose but wages did not keep pace with them. The working and living conditions were shocking, social services were almost non-existent and the spectre of periodic unemployment was a constant source of worry. The new freedom to strike, given by the Trades Disputes Act, led to a period of industrial unrest and a move towards syndicalism, especially amongst unskilled workers.

A railway strike in 1911, paralysed a large part of the country and in the following year **850 000 miners** went on strike for a minimum wage, all over the country, of 5 shillings a day. Many other industries were affected and the coal export trade received a blow from which it never recovered. One feature of time was the development of **sympathetic strikes**, whilst another was the formation, in 1914, of the **Triple Alliance** of miners, railwaymen and transport workers.

Much of the union's activity during this period was directed towards increasing Labour's representation in parliament. This resulted in the development of the **Labour Representation Committee** (1900), which in 1906 became known as the **Labour Party** and began to increase its number of seats in parliament, sometimes co-operating with the Liberal Party in a Lib-Lab Pact. Thus for the first time there was a Labour Party able to influence affairs.

Ireland

Although Conservative 'kindness' in Ireland had brought prosperity, it had not 'killed Home Rule'. In 1910, it became obvious that as a result of the election, the Liberals would be dependent upon the Irish vote to pass the Parliament Bill. **John Redmond**, the Irish Nationalist leader saw the possibility of gaining Home Rule in exchange for support against the Lords. Asquith, the Liberal leader had no choice but to bring in a Home Rule Bill in 1912.

Ulster now became the stumbling block to Home Rule. Ulster was protestant and had a history of hatred of the Catholic South. Moreover, Ulster had industries that she felt the South coveted. This hatred was inflamed by the English Unionists, who were determined not to suffer a third defeat at the hands of the Liberals, and who expected that opposition from Ulster would wreck the Liberal plan for Home Rule.

Sir Edward Carson, an M.P. and former Attorney-General, agreed to lead the Irish Unionists. He prepared to oppose Home Rule in Parliament and to make a stand against it in Ulster by setting up a provisional government, enlisting volunteers and arming them. He was supported in this course by English Unionists, notably Lord Birkenhead. This was in line with the policy laid down by Lord Randolph Churchill, who had written, 'Ulster will fight and Ulster will be right'.

Asquith was in a dilemma. He could not drop Home Rule, neither could he force Ulster to accept it. He was weak enough to let the **Ulster Volunteers** flourish and to be matched by the **Irish (Nationalist) Volunteers**. It seemed as if the Home Rule Bill's acceptance by the Crown would be the signal for civil war in Ireland. Things were made worse by the fact that British officers were pro-Ulster in sympathy. An attempt to excuse officers who lived in Ulster from any fighting, was misunderstood and ended with a declaration at the **Curragh**, from officers of the 3rd Cavalry Brigade, that they would rather accept dismissal than be ordered North. The War Office assured them that they would not be so ordered.

A special conference tried to get an agreed solution to the problem, but failed on the day of Austria's ultimatum to Serbia. So the Home Rule Act was suspended for the duration of the war. Many Irishmen from the South as well as the North fought in the British army, but the **Sinn Fein rebellion of Easter 1916**, mounted with German aid, served to remind the English that Home Rule was still an issue with the Irish.

Imperial affairs

Entente with Russia (1907) supplemented the earlier entente with France by a clearing up of disputes with Russia. Both Russia and Britain undertook not to encroach in disputed territory and agreed to divide Persia into spheres of influence with a buffer area between them.

New Zealand formally assumed the status of a Dominion, though this did not require any constitutional change, as it had been fully self governing for some time (1907).

Lord Cromer retired (1907) after 24 years' service in Egypt. He had carried through many reforms and lifted many burdens from the peasants, whilst being continually hampered by France, Turkey and Germany. His retirement seemed to **Egyptian Nationalists** to be the right time for a British withdrawal, but the British felt that Egypt would be very important strategically, in the event of a war and that the British presence was necessary in Egypt.

In the **Transvaal** and the **Orange Free State**, the preliminary period of representative government was waived and full self government was granted (1907). This led on to the **Union of South Africa**, which came into force in 1910. The intention was that Cape Colony, Natal, Transvaal and the O.F.S. should become a federation, but the provincial legislatures had no inalienable rights.

The Imperial Conference (1907) was the new name adopted at that date for Colonial Conferences. Australia decided to form a navy of her own. It was also decided to create an Imperial General Staff. A separate Dominions Department was created in the Colonial Office.

At a **Defence Conference** in 1909 New Zealand and Australia offered naval help to Britain, in view of the growing threat from Germany, while Canada formed a squadron of her own.

British Malaya was extended in 1909 by the transfer of a number of states to British rule from the nominal control of Siam. The states were made separate protectorates and did not join the federated Malay States.

In India, a loyal reception was given to George V, in person, at the **Delhi Durbar**. Delhi became the new capital of India and the unpopular partition of Bengal was reversed (1911). This show of loyalty provoked an attempt to assassinate the Viceroy, Lord Hardinge, on his state entry to Delhi.

Johore, a wealthy state in Malaya, had been friendly with Britain and in 1914, it formally became one of the Federated Malay States, with its own British Adviser.

Foreign affairs

When Sir Edward Grey became Foreign Secretary, Britain was in the process of emerging from isolation and her latest entente, with France, was being severely tested by Germany, who was insisting upon a European conference at **Algeciras**. Grey continued to support France and logically made friends with France's other ally, Russia.

An **Anglo-Russian agreement** was reached in 1907, whereby differences over Afghanistan and Tibet were settled by a promise of no further expansion. The chief clause concerned the division of Persia into 3 spheres of influence: the Russian one in the North, British in the South and a central buffer zone. Its conclusion meant that the **Triple Entente** of Britain, France and Russia faced the **Triple Alliance** of Germany, Austria and Italy.

The Bosnian Crisis (1908) was a diplomatic defeat for Russia. Exploiting the difficulties of Turkey, Austria annexed Bosnia and Herzegovina without prior warning to Russia. Germany backed Austria and Russia not wanting war, agreed. Russia now felt the need to strengthen the Entente.

Anglo-German Naval Rivalry was intensified with the appearance of the 'Dreadnought', in 1906. The scare that Germany would achievè parity, forced the government to lay down 8 dreadnoughts in 1908.

Right up to 1914, all attempts to come to terms with Germany foundered on her refusal to call off the **naval arms race**.

The Agadir incident (1911), was a warning that Germany had not abandoned her claims in Morocco. When the French sent troops into Fez to protect Europeans and to extend their influence, Germany sent the 'Panther' to Agadir and claimed compensation. After a warning from Britain (Lloyd George's Mansion House Speech) Germany withdrew with some minor strips of African territory as compensation.

Naval Arrangements with France (1912) meant that Britain concentrated her battle fleet in the North Sea, Channel and

Atlantic, leaving France to guard the Mediterranean. This arrangement gave Britain a moral obligation to help France in the event of a German attack.

Haldane's Army Reforms made provision for the rapid mobilization of the army in the event of war. Thus in 1914 a British Expeditionary Force was rapidly organized and dispatched to aid France. The Territorial Army was formed to act as a reserve of troops.

Italy's War with Turkey (1911–12) followed the Austrian example of taking advantage of Turkey's weakness after the revolt of the **Young Turks**; her seizure of Tripoli encouraged the Balkan States of Serbia, Bulgaria, Greece and Montenegro to form the **Balkan League** under the lead of Venizelos and to attack Turkey (1912).

In the **first Balkan War**, Turkey was routed and her European territory, limited to a coastal strip, by the **Treaty of London** of 1913. The members of the Balkan League quarrelled about the way the spoils were shared. Bulgaria, having borne the brunt of the fighting, felt disgruntled at her share and attacked her former ally, Serbia, in the **second Balkan War** (1913). Serbia's success and consequent enlargement aroused a longing, in her peoples to free their brothers, in Bosnia, from the Austrian yoke. This caused anger in Austria and contributed to the outbreak of the 1914 war.

The Sarajevo Crisis (June 1914) brought matters to a head. The murder of Franz Ferdinand, the Austrian Archduke, together with his wife, by a Bosnian Serb gave Austria the chance to deal with Serbia before she became any stronger. A stiff ultimatum to Serbia was, surprisingly, accepted in all its main points, but Austria, confident of German support, determined to crush Serbia even at the risk of European War.

The Road to War:

July 28   Austria declared war on Serbia.

August 1   Germany declared war on Russia.
           France mobilized to help Russia.

August 3   Germany declared war on France.

Grey, the British Foreign Secretary proposed a conference, but although Russia, France and Italy approved, Germany refused. Germany still hoped for British neutrality, but though Grey held that we were not bound to go to war unless the German fleet attacked France, we were morally bound to support France. **The violation of Belgium** by Germany, contrary to her neutral status, signalled Britain's entry into the war.

August 4   Britain declared war on Germany.

Parliamentary Reform

The system in 1815

The system was out of date: it had not been altered to take note of the changes brought about by the Industrial and Agricultural Revolutions. It had existed in England with very little change, since Tudor times. In Scotland and Ireland, the system dated back to the Acts of Union, 1707 and 1800, respectively.

There were **religious disabilities** for Roman Catholics, Nonconformists, Jews and atheists.

The distribution of seats was unfair. Of the 658 members of the lower house, 513 represented English and Welsh constituencies but only 100 represented Ireland and 45 Scotland. Each English **county** sent two members (this goes back to the 13th century when there were two knights from every shire). The Welsh counties sent one member each.

By far the majority of members represented **boroughs**. They dated mostly from Medieval times, although the Tudors had created many in the Royal Duchy of Cornwall (Cornwall sent 44 members as compared with 45 for the whole of Scotland). Boroughs created or enlarged since the reign of James I, had no separate representation. 70% of members represented constituencies south of a line from the Wash to the Bristol Channel. Some boroughs had declined in size but still sent two members. In some cases, one man had the right to nominate the members, since he was the only elector—these were called 'pocket' or 'nomination' boroughs. Other boroughs where the number of voters was small enough for them to be bribed, were known as 'rotten' boroughs. The system was so absurd that large towns like Manchester, Leeds, Stoke, Oldham and Birmingham were not separately represented.

The franchise (right to vote) was restricted to only about 500 000 out of a population of some 15 000 000. The **county constituencies** had a uniform franchise—owners of land worth forty shillings a year. In **borough constituencies**, the franchise was a matter of local custom. In Corporation Boroughs, only members of the corporation could vote: in Freeman Boroughs only freemen of the borough: in Scot and Lot Boroughs the vote went to householders paying scot and lot (a kind of rate): in Burgage Boroughs, ownership of designated properties gave the right: in 'Potwalloper' Boroughs, the vote went to anyone owning a room with a hearth where a pot could be boiled.

The landed gentry controlled the House of Commons as well as the House of Lords. They were the patrons of 'pocket' boroughs: they influenced the voting in Rotten Boroughs by intimidation or bribery: the County voters tended to follow the example of the local gentry who were the leaders of society.

Corruption was widespread and not confined to elections. Electors sold their votes: owners of 'pocket' boroughs sold seats: once elected, members sold their votes for positions.

Open voting on the hustings, where a vote had to be called out openly, encouraged corruption, since it was easy to discover how a man voted and so bribe or intimidate him. Crowds who were partisan could also affect the voting in these conditions (as in 1832).

Demands for reform

In 1785, **Pitt the Younger** had introduced a measure of parliamentary reform, which he had had to abandon, but the demand for reform was kept alive over a period of nearly fifty years by **Grey** and **Russell**. At times the agitation verged on rioting, as at Peterloo and the agitation for the 1832 Bill. Strange bedfellows e.g. **Hunt and Bentham** advocated reform, symptomatic of the workers and middle classes who felt that parliamentary reform was the key that would unlock the door to a whole host of desirable reforms.

The ideas and influence of the **French** and **American Revolutions** also encouraged the demand for this reform.

There were of course those who opposed reform. They pointed out that the old system had enabled **men of genius** to rise to the top at a very early age. The Younger Pitt was cited as an example:

'A sight to make surrounding nations stare,

A kingdom trusted to a schoolboy's care'. Others pointed out that Britain under its old constitution had been able to oppose **Napoleon**, at times unaided, and to hold out until victory was assured. Again our constitution was held up as the envy of the world; the subject of **Montesquieu's** work and the example of the **Founding Fathers**, in America, in their attempts to ensure that their country should be 'safe from democracy'. Some people felt that an extension of the franchise to the middle classes, would strengthen the ruling classes and **postpone the need** for any great changes.

The **manufacturing** and **commercial classes** who had increased in numbers and importance during the Industrial Revolution were the main factor. They were determined to end the monopoly of power and influence that the landed gentry had enjoyed for so long. No one could deny the corruption that existed. The rotten borough of **Grampound** had been disfranchised by parliament in 1821, because of the notorious venality of its electors (about 50 in number). The two seats were given to Yorkshire because it was by far the largest county.

Religious disabilities

The Test and Corporation Acts date from the reign of Charles II. They prohibited nonconformists from holding office under the state or in a town corporation. In fact, many dissenters had evaded these acts and had been exempted from punishment by an annual Act of Indemnity. Now, Lord John Russell introduced a bill repealing these acts. The bill passed and nonconformist disabilities were removed from the statute book.

The Penal Laws against the catholics were strongly resented. This was especially so, since the Irish had been promised a Catholic Relief Act at the time of the Union (1800). The problem became acute after the **County Clare election**, when O'Connell, having been elected, was refused entry to parliament because of catholic religion. Wellington became convinced that to continue to refuse O'Connell his seat would mean a rebellion. The time was ripe for **a Catholic Relief Act** (1829) to end the many disabilities that Catholics suffered including the right to be a member of parliament. The posts of sovereign, regent, Lord Chancellor and Lord Lieutenant of Ireland remained closed to Catholics.

Other disabilities e.g. those of the Jews, remained.

The Reform Bill of 1832

The First Reform Bill (March 1831), introduced by Lord John Russell, suggested sweeping changes. Fifty boroughs were to lose both their members and fifty others were to lose one. The list of doomed boroughs was greeted with disbelief. Great speeches by Macauley, warned of the danger of delay. 'Reform that you may preserve', he suggested. The bill passed its second reading by a majority of one, but was defeated in its Committee Stage. Grey persuaded the reluctant William IV to agree to a dissolution so that he could go to the country.

The General Election (May 1831) saw enthusiastic mobs at the hustings, demanding reform and frightening electors into voting for the Whigs. They were returned with a 136 majority.

The Second Reform Bill (June 1831), was very similar to the first and it quickly passed through all stages in the Commons. Its defeat in the Lords by a majority of 41, led to uproar throughout the country which reached a peak in Nottingham, where the mob burnt the castle and in Bristol where the Mansion House was fired.

The Third Reform Bill (December 1831), passed the Commons in March 1832 but was severely amended in the Committee stage of the House of Lords. When the king refused Grey's request to create enough Whig peers to pass the bill, he resigned and Wellington, one-time hero of Waterloo, tried to form a ministry. He became the most hated man in the country. His windows were smashed. The crowds chanted slogans such as, 'To stop the Duke, go for gold' and 'The bill, the whole bill and nothing but the bill'. Wellington had to concede failure and **Grey** returned with the king's promise to create the necessary peers.

The Bill was passed, finally, without the creation of new peers because Wellington and one hundred peers (including the bishops) refrained from voting so that the bill gained sufficient votes to proceed for the **Royal Assent** (June 1832).

The terms of the act were:

1. Rotten and pocket boroughs were swept away, with boroughs with a population of less than 2 000 losing both their seats and with boroughs with a population between 2 and 4 thousand, losing one of their seats.

2. The 143 seats thus available for redistribution were given to large counties (65 seats), large towns (44 seats), smaller towns (21 seats), Scotland (8 seats), Ireland (5 seats).

3. All boroughs now had a uniform qualification for the vote i.e. possession or occupation of a house worth £10 per annum.

4. In the Counties, the 40 shilling freeholder retained the vote; the £10 per annum long leaseholder (copyholder) and the £50 per annum short leaseholder were given the vote.

Significance of the Act was:

1. The number of voters was increased to over 650 000.

2. Landowners gradually lost influence.

3. Middle classes obtained the vote and slowly began to appear in parliament.

4. The workers gained nothing. Some even lost the vote. The leaders of both parties regarded this extension of the franchise as final. The workers now turned to movements such as trade

unions and the Chartists for the fulfilment of their hopes.

5. This was a first faltering step towards democracy.

6. It opened the way for an era of reform.

Chartism and parliamentary reform

Much of the disappointment of the workers at the terms of the Reform Act (1832), found expression in Chartism, a movement which aimed to present a charter to the government in the form of a petition, containing a political programme of six points:

1. A vote for all adult males.

2. Voting by secret ballot.

3. The abolition of the property qualification for M.Ps.

4. Payment of M.Ps.

5. Equal electoral districts.

6. Annual elections.

The London Working Men's Association (1836), with William Lovett, as secretary and Francis Place, as chief adviser, drafted the charter and launched it in 1838. It was to be presented to the Commons accompanied by a mass petition. For this purpose a **Convention** was arranged. This met in 1839, but found that only half a million signatures had been collected.

Further propaganda was arranged with torchlight processions and monster meetings. Soon the number of signatures was estimated at $1\frac{1}{4}$ million, but the movement attracted many cranks with their own pet schemes and leaders who rejected the constitutional ways of William Lovett.

Parliament's rejection of the petition in 1839, and again in 1842 shows that it thought the proposals revolutionary and it is true that the movement got into the hands of the 'physical force' section of the movement, led by **Feargus O'Connor**, but it showed the nation that the workers were dissatisfied with having no say in the running of the country. It showed the need for more reform.

As **Peel's budgets** began to take effect, the economic causes of Chartism were removed and as Palmerston emerged as the most influential man of the time, parliamentary reform became a dead letter with all but a few determined Chartists and a few radicals like Bright. However it is to Disraeli that we must look for the next step forward in parliamentary reform.

Disraeli's reforms (1858)

In the second Derby-Disraeli ministry (1858–9), some minor acts were passed on the subject of parliamentary reform:

1. Jews were allowed in parliament.
2. The property qualification for M.Ps. was removed.

In addition, a Fancy Franchise Bill failed to pass the Commons.

Russell, Bright, Gladstone

Lord John Russell, having introduced the Reform Bill of 1832, in face of Chartist pressure, declared that his bill was 'final'. For this he received the nick-name of 'Finality Jack'. In spite of this he again took up the cause of parliamentary reform in 1852 and 1854. Although these proposals failed, he again brought up the matter with Gladstone in 1866, when Robert Lowe and his **Adullamites** went against their party in opposing the moderate reform measure introduced in the Commons by **Gladstone** in 1866. However the death of Palmerston in 1865 had brought the growing demand for reform to a head. It was supported by the trade unions and that great advocate of parliamentary reform, **John Bright**, who was convinced that the workers, if enfranchised, would use their votes to support a more moral foreign policy than that of Palmerston. Lowe's action ensured the rejection of the bill, which would have added a further 300 000 to the electorate. It also gave the opportunity for the Conservatives to form a ministry, although they were in a minority.

The Second Reform Act (1867)

Working class agitation now flared up in favour of reform; a crowd broke the railings to hold a meeting in Hyde Park, when the authorities closed the gates. **Bright** was again agitating for reform and it was obvious that it must come. Gambling that a Conservative Act would win them the votes of the workers and in line with his early radical beliefs, **Disraeli** persuaded Derby to agree to a new reform bill. Disraeli proposed to give the vote to the £6 per annum householder, in the boroughs and the £20 leaseholder in the counties. As the bill passed through the various stages in the Commons it became more democratic than its authors intended and also more democratic than the Russell-Gladstone measure of the previous year. There was even a proposal to give the vote to women, though it was met with scorn and received only 73 votes. In its final form, **Disraeli's act** gave the vote to the lodger, in unfurnished rooms, who paid a rental of £10 per annum, putting him on a par with the householder in **borough constituencies**. In the **counties**, £12 per annum leaseholders gained the vote. At the same time 45 seats were taken from the smaller boroughs and given to the larger counties and towns. In addition, nine new boroughs were represented in parliament. Lord Derby described it as, 'a leap in the dark'; and Carlyle likened it to 'shooting Niagara'; while it led Robert Lowe to his famous dictum that, 'We must educate our masters'. Disraeli's boast to have 'dished the Whigs' proved untrue, for at the **election of 1868**, the new voters (more than half the total) gave their votes, not to Disraeli but to Gladstone. However, the act had given the vote to the artisan class in the towns and their interests had to be taken into account in future legislation.

Gladstone's reforms

Gladstone rewarded the faith of the workers with a number of reforms that concerned parliament:

The Ballot Act (1872) swept away the old system of open voting at the hustings and with it much of the bribery and intimidation at elections. Since the ballot papers were now placed in a sealed ballot box and not opened until the count, it was no longer possible for the mob or the employer or landowner to see how a man had voted. An unexpected result of the act was that it enabled many Irish voters to ignore the wishes of the landlord and to elect M.Ps. in favour of Home Rule.

The Corrupt Practices Act (1883) was designed to prevent bribery and intimidation at elections by limiting election expenses and specifying the purposes on which the money could be spent. It closely defined certain offences at elections and required the candidate's agent to submit accounts of expenses.

The Representation of the People Act (1884) is better known as the 3rd Reform Act. It enfranchised householders in counties as in boroughs, and occupiers of land or buildings worth £10 per annum. It also gave the vote to servants who lived apart from their masters. It did not give the vote to servants who lived in their master's house nor to sons who lived with their parents. Neither was there any arrangement for people travelling about to cast their vote. It increased the number of electors to 5 000 000, largely by including the lower paid workers in town and country.

The Redistribution of Seats Act (1885) aimed at equal electoral districts and single member constituencies, on a basis of one M.P. for every 50 000 of the population. Boroughs with less than 15 000 inhabitants lost both their members; those with between 15 000 and 50 000 were to have only one member. Large boroughs and counties were to be divided up into single member constituencies, though 22 towns and some universities still retained two members. As a result of the Act, the Irish Nationalists increased their seats and the Whigs lost many of theirs.

Liberals (1906–14)

Much of Campbell-Bannerman's legislation, including a **plural voting bill** was rejected by the Lords. As a result the Commons clashed with the Lords and determined to limit their power.

They therefore introduced the **Parliament Act** which:

1. Limited the Lords' power to hold up a money bill to 28 days.
2. Limited their power to hold up other bills to 2 years.
3. Limited the life of parliament to five years instead of seven.

This act of 1911 has been amended in 1949, so that a bill can be delayed for only one year.

The Payment of M.Ps. was introduced in 1911. They were given a salary of £400 per annum so that the working class could be represented by workers, who hitherto had not been able to afford to be an M.P. This was also introduced to make up for the loss to workers' representatives as a result of the Osborne Judgement in the House of Lords.

So we see that in the 100 years from 1815 to 1914, great steps were taken towards establishing a democratic system of parliamentary elections. What is perhaps most surprising to us today, is the list of reforms that still remained to be done:

1. Women were not allowed to vote until 1918 and even then it was only women over 30. Those in their twenties had to wait until 1928 for the vote (even then it was referred to as 'the flapper vote').
2. Certain men e.g. grown-up sons living at home and servants living with their master, also were given the vote in 1918.
3. Certain people, e.g. university graduates retained a second vote right down to after the 2nd World War. In 1948 all plural voting was abolished.

Education

The development of education in the nineteenth century is a story of considerable achievement. At the beginning of the period, the state played no part in providing education but by the First World War, there was a compulsory system of elementary education, with schools available throughout the land. On top of this there was a system of scholarships whereby the able sons and daughters of poor parents could proceed, by means of scholarships, first to secondary school and then on to university.

Education in 1815

In England, after the defeat of Napoleon, there was no state system of education: indeed the idea of educating the poor seemed dangerous and revolutionary to the ruling classes, while the employers feared that education would rob them of the cheap labour on which they depended. However, for a number of reasons it seemed desirable that the workers should be educated:

1. The increasing use of machinery in the mills made it necessary to give some technical training to workers.
2. Businesses could not be run efficiently without someone who could read and write and do some form of accounts.
3. The new towns lacked a parish church to act as a centre of religion and it was felt that the poor should receive some instruction in religion.
4. There was a growing feeling that if the workers were to have a say in the running of the country by means of a vote, then they should be educated to use their vote wisely.

The existing schools seemed unlikely to expand much without aid from the government. These **existing schools** were:

1. **Public schools** which catered for the sons of the aristocracy were run for profit and were very expensive.
2. **Old established grammar schools** were few and far between; they were preoccupied with Latin and failed to cater for or appeal to any but a narrow clientele.
3. **Governesses** taught the daughters of the aristocracy and the aspiring middle classes.
4. **Dame schools** minded rather than taught the children of those who preferred to work and pay someone else to look after their children.

5. **Sunday schools**, started by Robert Raikes of Gloucester, in 1870, taught poor children to read so that they might learn to read the scriptures. As the name suggests they met only on Sundays and did not make a very great impact.

6. **Religious bodies** began to provide educational facilities for the poor, with Church of England schools in rivalry with Nonconformist schools, so that it is difficult to escape the conclusion that they were proselytizing. The pioneers were Dr. **Andrew Bell** who started C. of E. (National schools) and **Joseph Lancaster**, a Quaker, who set up Lancasterian schools in South London which later led to the British and Foreign School Society. These voluntary bodies were not state aided and relied upon private subscription and endowments. Both used the older pupils to act as monitors and to teach the younger children. This system had the great advantage of being cheap.

Whatever the drawbacks of these schools (and their sectarianism was a source of conflict throughout the century), they provided the foundation upon which the state system was to be built.

State Aid

In 1833, Parliament took a first step towards a state system of education by making a **grant of £20 000** to the voluntary societies. The grant became annual and increased until by 1839 it had become £30 000. To supervise this spending of government money, a **Committee of the Privy Council** for Education was set up, which proved to be the forerunner of the Board of Education. This was followed by a system of **inspection of schools** and the **pupil-teacher system**. The government grant steadily increased, reaching £900 000 in 1858 but the bulk of the population remained illiterate.

To improve matters, Robert Lowe, head of the Education Department introduced a system of '**payment by results**', which meant that the amount of grant a school would receive would depend upon the performance of the school in a series of examinations carried out by government inspectors. The system was abused by schools and fell into disrepute.

After Disraeli's 'Leap in the Dark', Robert Lowe insisted that, 'We must educate our masters'. It was felt that if the workers were to have the vote (and few voices were openly raised against this now), then they must be given the opportunity to be educated. The voluntary schools still catered for only half the child population and left 10 000 parishes without a school.

The realization that England was lagging behind other nations in education and the demands of industry, the civil service and the armed forces for educated personnel made it essential to fill the gaps in our educational system.

Forster's Elementary Education Act (1870)

This act, passed in Gladstone's first ministry, provided elementary education for children of the poor. It tried to make school available for every child in the land. To do so, it set up a **new state school** where no voluntary school existed. The money was to come from a special rate and the schools were to be run by a school board, elected by ratepayers. It catered for children between the ages of five and thirteen and each board could decide for itself whether to make education compulsory. There was a fee of about 2 pence per week although parents unable to afford this could be excused. In practice parents and pupils often conspired to defeat the attendance officers (school board men). The schools were to give religious instruction of non-sectarian nature and were to be paid for out of the rates with the aid of government grants.

Voluntary schools were to receive increased government grants. In all schools, a child could be withdrawn from Scripture lessons at the request of the parents. This was the **Cowper-Temple clause** which caused a great deal of argument.

Nonconformists complained about the increased state aid to the numerous C. of E. schools which were still the only schools in many areas.

The Church of England complained that the board schools were not sufficiently religious.

An act of parliament in Disraeli's second ministry made attendance at school compulsory—no longer leaving the local school boards to decide for themselves. It was impossible to insist fully upon this until, in 1891, Salisbury's ministry made education **free as well as compulsory** and provided the money by means of a new government grant.

In 1899, the **Board of Education** was set up and in 1902, its control was tightened when the Balfour Act abolished the school boards and placed schools under the new **local authorities**— county councils, county borough councils, certain large borough councils and urban district councils.

A new dimension was given to state education by **Balfour's Act** when it set up secondary schools to which able children of poor parents might aspire, by means of a scholarship.

Secondary education

With the turn of the century, progressive school boards had begun to provide '**Higher Grade Schools**' (or sometimes classes) for their brighter pupils whose parents could not afford to send them to grammar schools. The expenditure of ratepayer's money on these 'Higher Grade Schools' was declared unauthorized following a court case in 1900. In 1902, therefore, Balfour introduced his act to make secondary education a question for the state.

The new secondary schools were to be run by the County Councils with the aid of a government grant. New schools were built and old grammar schools helped with grants. It was possible for pupils to pass from elementary school to grammar school, usually at the age of eleven. In 1907, the Liberals required all secondary schools, in receipt of government grants, to allocate at least 25 per cent of their places, free to scholarship pupils from the elementary schools. This ensured the success of the grammar schools and strengthened the **educational ladder** by which able pupils might pass from the elementary to the grammar school. Further scholarships made it possible for the brightest children to go on from there to university. In this way a sense of entity was woven into the fabric of state education.

Social Service in state schools

In 1906, the **Provision of Meals Act** empowered Local Education Authorities to feed children who came to school hungry by the provision of free meals. This was because of concern for the health of the urban population in general and those children in particular who suffered from rickets caused by calcium deficiency.

In 1907, **the Medical Inspection Act** brought elementary school children under the medical inspection teams of the local health authorities. This was later extended by the provision of special school clinics and by the inclusion of secondary school children in the scheme.

Public schools

Public schools were bad in most respects in the first quarter of the nineteenth century, with a continual state of war between the staff and the boys which reached a peak at Winchester College where troops were called in to end a riot by the boys. The improvements were largely the work of a few **reforming**

headmasters. Perhaps the best known of these headmasters who raised standards at the Public schools was **Thomas Arnold**. He was appointed as headmaster of Rugby School in 1827 and changed the system there into an organized training for adult life. Working through a body of prefects, he inspired the boys with his own ideal of 'a Christian gentleman' as immortalized in 'Tom Brown's Schooldays'. Gradually his work improved standards in public schools generally through the efforts of 'old boys' who became headmasters and others who imitated his ideas.

Another reforming headmaster was **Samuel Butler**, headmaster of Shrewsbury School. He increased the standard of the school's scholarship, but even he disapproved of Charles Darwin spending his time in a Chemistry laboratory when he might have been studying the Classics.

Edward Thring, headmaster of Uppingham School from 1853 to 1887, raised it to the highest rank in numbers and repute. He rebelled against mere routine and attached great value to music, drawing and the decoration of the schoolrooms. He was also keen to match the interests of his pupils to the studies and games that the school provided.

Thus the public schools catered for the new, ambitious middle classes as well as their traditional clientele by a new emphasis on **character building** and self-reliance. Their success may be judged by the way their number increased in the nineteenth century with the addition of such schools as Marlborough, Malvern and Haileybury.

Universities

In the early part of the nineteenth century, England could boast only of the two ancient universities—**Oxford and Cambridge**. A test of religion reserved admission and fellowships to members of the Church of England. Teaching was usually badly organized and many of the fellows were idle.

The founding of **University College**, in London (1828) to provide education without any religious test earned the title of the 'Godless College' for that institution and provoked the founding of **King's College** by the Anglicans. The two, together, formed the **University of London** in 1836, though they retained their separate identities.

Durham University was formed in 1832 and **Manchester** in 1880, to be followed in the decade after 1900, by Birmingham, Liverpool, Leeds, Sheffield and Bristol. Known as the '**red-brick**' universities, they were situated in industrial centres and tended to specialize in commerce and technology.

Reform in universities was slow, but government action in Gladstone's first ministry came with the **Universities Test Act** (1871) which abolished the religious test for entry and for fellowships. Later improvements included the addition of modern scientific subjects to the curriculum and changes in the way the college endowments were used.

Thus, with competition, the ancient universities were forced to improve their ways and play a greater part in the life of the nation. At present, they are being forced by the movement for women's liberation and the sex discrimination Act to move towards equal opportunities and treatment for young women.

Outside the universities, there was a growing demand for **adult education** from the working classes. This demand was met to some extent by the appearance of Mechanics Institutes (the first founded in London by Dr. Birkbeck, later became a college of the University of London). There was also a growth of **polytechnics** which developed in London from classes for street urchins under the Adelphi arches and removed to a disused building in Regent Street. Their aim was to develop industrial skills and they received grants from the London County Council under the Technical Instruction Act of 1889. Some have now developed as universities e.g. Northampton Polytechnic became the City University.

A growing number of **evening schools** also developed especially providing instruction in commercial subjects.

Education for girls

Education for girls, in the first half of the century was almost non existent. Even the daughters of the wealthy and influential were usually educated at home by a governess while their brothers were sent to school. They were taught subjects which would help them to win (or keep) a husband and enable them to run a household. However, the second half of the century saw rapid developments in the provision of higher education for girls to fit them for a more important role in society.

The Christian Socialists, Frederick Kingsley and Frederick Maurice took the first step in this direction when they founded Queen's College and Bedford College in London (1848–9). Among their first pupils were Frances Buss and Dorothea Beale.

Miss Buss founded the North London Collegiate School for Girls, in 1850 and in 1870 this was handed over to trustees and became the Girls' Public Day School Trust. Using the North London Collegiate as a model, they founded schools throughout the country (including the Manchester High School for Girls, 1874). These schools provided girls with an education previously kept for boys. The curriculum included classics, history and mathematics and the teaching was of a very high standard.

Miss Beale became Principal of Cheltenham Ladies' College in 1858 and pioneered boarding school education for girls.

These two overcame a great deal of prejudice and ridicule and devoted their lives to the cause of education for girls. They both gave evidence before the 'Endowed Schools Enquiry Commission' in 1865. The report on the education of girls attracted wide attention and stimulated a demand for **university education** for women.

Only London University admitted women to examinations and degrees but the provincial universities followed suit. Oxford and Cambridge Universities still excluded women.

In 1869, Emily Davies founded **Girton College** for women at Hitchin.

In 1871, **Newnham College** opened in Cambridge itself, with Miss Clough as its first head. In 1872, Girton moved to Cambridge. These Cambridge colleges were shortly followed by colleges in Oxford:

In 1878, **Lady Margaret Hall** was founded.

In 1879, **Somerville College** was founded.

In 1886, **St. Hugh's** and in 1893 **St. Hilda's** followed.

Women were not admitted as members of the universities, but were allowed to attend lectures and take examinations. After some outstanding performances in examinations, women were finally allowed to take their degrees after the First World War.

Elementary education, as provided for in Forster's Act, made no distinction as between boys and girls and it was at this end of the educational spectrum that unspectacular but solid progress was made. Girls went to school and mixed with other girls. New standards were imparted to them. With the appearance of the typewriter as a practical proposition, appearing on the market in 1874 (Remington), more attractive career prospects opened for girls and this in turn boosted the desire on the part of girls to be educated.

Grammar schools, too, at the turn of the century, following Balfour's Act, provided for girls and co-educational and girls' grammar schools began to teach girls in readiness for the professions, for teacher-training and for the universities.

Trade Unions

The Younger Pitt, during the wars against Napoleon, came to identify reform with the excesses of the French Revolution. The reformers, who adopted the language of revolutionaries, made people equate them with the enemy and **Pitt's Combination Acts** of 1799 and 1800 seemed reasonable as a war-time measure. The acts forbade any combinations of workmen to act together to improve their wages, reduce working hours or otherwise change their conditions of labour. With the return to peace in 1815, the acts were not repealed. The government saw demands for reform as proof that the workers were preparing for revolution in this country and far from repealing Pitt's acts, they strengthened them.

Trade unions—1824 to 1834

The repeal of the Combination Acts in 1824, was largely the work of **Francis Place**. A breeches-maker, turned tailor, Place used his shop as a centre of radical activity: such men as Sir Francis Burdett (a radical M.P.), Joseph Hume (another radical M.P.), Jeremy Benthan (the Utilitarian) might be seen there.

When Hume was appointed to a parliamentary committee to enquire into the law relating to combinations of workmen, Place persuaded him to call before the committee, witnesses who had been rehearsed by Place to reiterate that workers only wished to combine because it was forbidden to do so. The committee reported in favour of **repealing the Combination Acts** and this was duly carried out in 1824.

Trade unions, hitherto disguised as Friendly Societies, now flourished and new ones began to appear. A **wave of strikes** broke out among unions anxious to try their wings and to claim their share of the profits of the trade boom. When the boom gave way to a slump, the masters tried to reduce wages and to blame the strikes on the repeal of the Combination Acts. Parliament prepared to re-enact the laws, but Place prepared evidence as to the nature of booms and slumps and the **acts were re-imposed** only in a modified form. Trade unions remained legal and were allowed to bargain on behalf of their members providing no violence was involved. This act of 1825 left the position of unions unclear. Their isolation in small groups left them weak.

A national organization was seen by John Doherty, a spinner, as the main need if unions were to become effective. He formed the National Association for the Protection of Labour (1830) which achieved a membership of 100 000 from twenty different trades, by the end of the year. This scheme which had started with the Manchester cotton spinners and spread to other textile industries in the North, collapsed in 1831 through failure to co-ordinate the operations of its many members.

The Grand National Consolidated Trades Union, founded by Robert Owen in 1834, was the greatest and last of the efforts to form a national organization. It met with early success, attracting half a million members in a few weeks. It planned to unite the workers of all industries in a single union and thus to be in a position to call a **general strike**. Its aims went beyond the improvement of wages and working conditions; Owen planned that the workers should take over the control of industry. There was enthusiastic support from the workers who were suffering from the economic crisis and who were incensed by the failure of the 1832 Reform Act to reward the efforts of the workers by the vote. Owen's leadership was unable to prevent localized strikes and government action against many leaders under the conspiracy acts led the movement to fade away as quickly as it had grown up.

The Tolpuddle Martyrs were six Dorsetshire farm workers who tried to form a trade union and who were prosecuted with the full vigour of the law for administering illegal oaths. The oaths were nothing more than an initiation ceremony, common at the time, but the government was looking for a **scapegoat** and the men were sentenced to seven years' transportation. Although public opinion compelled their release some two years later, the lesson that it was dangerous to belong to a trade union was brought home and trade union activity died down. Many workers now gave their support to chartism or to the co-operative movement.

New Model unions

Unions continued in a small way among men in skilled trades who were better paid and who looked upon their union as a friendly society which collected subscriptions as an insurance against sickness rather than a means to build up a strike fund. They had paid officials and sought to negotiate better conditions. The best known of these unions was the **Amalgamated Society of Engineers** (1851) and this became a model for other unions to copy. Unskilled workers were not attracted to this form of union as they could not afford the subscriptions.

The Junta was a nickname given to the permanent secretaries of the New Model Unions, by their enemies, who thus compared them with a group of hated seventeenth century politicians with the same nickname. Led by **Robert Applegarth** of the Carpenters' Union, these men, centred in London, used their influence on the side of moderation. They worked to improve the law regarding trade unions and to create a less violent image for them. The latter aim received a set-back in 1866, when file grinders, on strike in Sheffield, attacked employers and 'blacklegs'. Their greatest achievement was the calling of the first Trades Union Congress (**T.U.C.**) in 1868. This developed into an annual meeting of trade unionists, on a national scale, to discuss topics of mutual interest. In turn the meeting led to a permanent body which acted as spokesman for the whole movement. Thus an elected body superseded the Junta and had a brief to advise members and to study the import of legislation affecting unions.

Trade unions under Gladstone and Disraeli

In the same year as the Second Reform Act (1867), a parliamentary commission was set up to enquire into trade unions. Their position was not clear. They had been legalized but their rights were ill-defined. Were they able to sue in law courts? Could they be sued? Could they strike? Could they act against any blacklegs? None of these points were clear. Gladstone made up his mind to settle the problem. His **Trade Union Act** of 1871 gave unions legal status: they could hold property; they could take legal action e.g. against absconding officials. This was welcomed by the unions.

His **Criminal Law Amendment Act** of the same year was not so well received. This recognized the right to strike but denied the right to picket even peacefully. The offences of 'molestation' and 'obstruction' were strictly defined. Since at this time trade unionists were always in a minority, a strike would not stand much chance of success if they were denied the right to picket.

Disraeli, in 1875, responded to working class agitation and introduced the **Conspiracy and Protection of Property Act**. This repealed Gladstone's Act and legalized picketing as long as it was peaceful.

A further act of the same year, made breach of contract on the part of a worker, a civil rather than a criminal offence. This

was the **Employers and Workmen Act**.
These acts strengthened the unions and by providing the strike weapon, paved the way for the formation of unskilled unions who were anxious to try out their powers.

New Unions

The Second Reform Act and Forster's Education Act gave the worker the vote and an elementary education. The same period saw a growth of socialism, a split in the Liberal Party which had hitherto been the hope of the workers and a period of unemployment which especially affected the unskilled worker. In these circumstances, **unskilled workers** formed unions of their own, more willing to strike and demonstrate than the New Model Unions. They also boasted a much greater membership.

Side by side with this new development in the trade union movement was the attempt to form a **political party** to represent the workers. The fusion of these two factors led to the formation of the Labour Party.

The New Unions were helped in their efforts by prominent members of the New Model Unions. **Tom Mann** and **John Burns**, as well as being trade unionists (Amalgamated Society of Engineers) were members of the **Social Democratic Federation** (founded by Hyndman in 1884). They complained that the unions were over-cautious and they helped to spread unionism to the unskilled workers.

The matchgirls' strike (1888), was encouraged by the appearance of an article by Mrs. Annie Besant. 700 girls, employed by Bryant & May, went on strike for better pay and working conditions. The success of the strike and the sympathy they received from the public encouraged other strikes.

The Gasworkers, employed by the South Metropolitan Gas Company, went on strike for an eight hour day. Their employers had to give way and other gas companies followed their lead (1889).

The London Dockers, led by Tom Mann, John Burns and Ben Tillet organized a complete shutdown of the London Docks, later the same year. On the verge of defeat, the dockers suddenly received help from sympathizers in Britain, in Europe and in Australia. They were thus able to hold out until they had achieved 'the dockers' tanner' and a minimum of four hours work at a time. The success of this strike led to an enormous increase in union membership.

The Taff Vale Judgement (1901) awarded damages of £42 000 to the Taff Vale Railway Company in respect of an action brought against the Amalgamated Society of Railway Servants who had called a strike. This was a serious blow to the unions who had believed that they were protected by law from such an action. It meant that their position built up on the acts of Gladstone and Disraeli was now in ruins. There were vigorous protests that the judges had virtually made a new law. It was to parliament that the workers had to turn for redress.

The Trade Disputes Act (1906) was introduced by the Liberal government, who were keen to have working class support. The act gave trade unions the protection from actions for damages which they had previously assumed they had.

The Labour Party

The parliamentary committee of the T.U.C. was slow to build up a party exclusive to workers. It worked with the Liberal Party to the extent of encouraging 'Lib-Lab' M.Ps. to accept the Liberal whip. **Robert Blatchford**, in his weekly 'The Clarion', urged the need for a Labour Party. The same stand was taken by **Keir Hardie**, the first independent Labour M.P. In 1893, Keir Hardie formed the Independent Labour Party. Nothing came of these moves until the T.U.C., in 1899, arranged for a conference to discuss the formation of a Labour Party.

The conference, representing the **Fabians**, the **S.D.F.** and the **I.L.P.** met in 1900 and established the **Labour Representation Committee**.

This new party, with Ramsay MacDonald as its secretary;
1. Formed its own whips.
2. Sponsored trade union members.
3. Cut the apron strings that tied it to the Liberals.

The Taff Vale Judgement gave the party new impetus; it marks the real beginning of the **Labour Party**.

In the election of 1906, the party gained 29 M.Ps. With a further 24 M.Ps. representing working class interests, a new political party was formed, helped by the **political levy** from the trade unions and the payment of a **salary** of £400 per annum to M.Ps. in 1911.

The Osborne Judgment(1909) was a temporary setback for the Labour Party. W.V. Osborne brought a successful action against his union, the Amalgamated Society of Railway Servants to restrain them from deducting the **political levy** (a small weekly sum collected from members to finance Labour M.Ps.).

The Trade Union Act (1913), restored the position by authorizing the levy on condition that the majority of the members of any union were in favour and that any member had **the right to 'contract out'** i.e. to refuse to pay the political levy. This levy remains an issue between the main parties today.

Syndicalism

In the opening years of the twentieth century, prices were rising and real wages were falling. Trade unions were stronger than ever before but hesitated to strike because of the Taff Vale Judgement. The passage of the **Trades Disputes Act** in 1906 was the signal for renewed industrial unrest.

In 1907 there was a prolonged dispute on the railways.

In 1909 and 1910 there were frequent strikes in mining areas.

The boilermakers and the cotton operatives were also involved in disputes. In the main, these strikes were unsuccessful but since parliamentary action seemed no more successful, the workers turned to direct action as advised by the **syndicalists** who looked on trade unions not merely as a means of collective bargaining but as a weapon with which to destroy the capitalist system.

They aimed to end private ownership and set up **workers' control**. Syndicalism found most support in South Wales, but the **Triple Alliance** of Miners, Railwaymen and Transport workers in 1913, planned to act together in a strike and foreshadowed the idea of the 'General Strike'. However, no opportunity to test their solidarity occurred before the outbreak of the First World War.

The Changing Status of Women

Although much still remained to be done, in 1914, it is quite surprising how the status of women did change in the hundred years from 1815 to 1914.

The position in 1815

In 1815, it was very much a case of '**woman's place is in the home**' especially for women of the middle and upper classes. Usually denied the opportunity of going to school, girls from the start, found their outlook limited by the home and their livelihood dependent upon their fathers. If they were educated, it would be by a governess, paid by their father and the object of the education would be to fit them for marriage. Women's role in early nineteenth century England was to be a loving mother to her children and an object of admiration to her husband. Marriage was still regarded as indissoluble and the home was regarded as the very rock upon which our civilization was built. The law saw marriage as binding two people together as one, and this being so, it was assumed that their interests were identical. This assumption, together with the belief that woman was the weaker, led to a legal code which, on marriage, made over a woman's property to her husband and also gave him control of any children. This seemed logical since man was believed to be more intellectual and to have more knowledge of the ways of the world. It provided the ideal set up for any man with ideas of marrying a woman for her money and no doubt explains why so many novels of the time harp on this theme.

The domestic life undoubtedly suited some women. They found fulfilment in motherhood and the running of a home. This was no easy task in a large household, with servants to manage, meals to plan, children to look after and social life to organize. Over and above this were the problems of regular pregnancies. Intellectually it was not demanding and some women, perhaps not fitted for the domestic scene, found it very restricting, and sought alternatives to this role. Such alternatives were few and might prove humiliating.

Women unsuccessful in finding a husband and unable to provide for themselves financially, might become a **dependent** in the home of a relative.

One respectable avenue of escape was to become a **gover-**

ness. It was not without an element of risk for it involved a change from dependence upon a father to dependence upon an employer and it might well prove to be a case of 'out of the frying pan into the fire.' There were difficulties too in that the status of a governess was not clearly defined. They might be treasured in one household and tolerated in another. They might be regarded as servants or as guests. It was certainly possible to make a tolerable life in this role and some were able to combine it with writing or a further round in the marriage stakes. It might also be possible to alternate it with some school teaching or to progress from one to the other. (e.g. Charlotte Brontë)

Writing was another avenue of escape but it was not easy. One had to be very good to make a success of it because of the prejudice that existed against women. Even writers like the Brontës found that it helped to adopt a masculine pseudonym.

Teaching posts for women in schools did exist, but they were few and far between, as well as being poorly paid.

Whatever the difficulties, there were women who overcame the greatest difficulties to follow an independent career:

Harriet Martineau overcame extreme ill health, deafness and bereavement, but still managed to start writing for a unitarian periodical.

The Brontë sisters were dogged by misfortune but persevered in their writing.

Elizabeth Barrett Browning had to deal with an over-possessive father. She wrote more popular poetry than her husband.

Elizabeth Fry, a quaker, formed the 'Association for the Improvement of Female Prisoners in Newgate' and later widened her interests to include hospital conditions and the care of the insane.

Others, such as **Christina Rosetti**, **Mrs. Ewings** and **George Eliot** despite the difficulty, were each writing in their own field around the mid-century.

But it was not only women from the upper classes who became famous. **Sarah Siddons**, who was born in the 'Shoulder of Mutton', public house, in Brecon, became a great actress, whose Lady Macbeth was recognized nationally as outstanding.

Working class women generally were having difficulties at this time (1815). Before industrialization, women worked hard. They had their families to rear; they kept house; they usually tended the garden and kept hens, besides helping out on the farm when things were busiest. In spite of all this, they were their own mistress; they held the family together. They were able to earn little luxuries by spinning (The husbands did the weaving and the children the carding). **Industrialization** brought other problems. They had to adapt to life in the new, insanitary towns; extra work had to be done in the factories where the work could not be done to suit the individual. It was 12 hour shifts or nothing. The children could not help their father on the farm or their mother about the house—they too, worked in the mills or climbed chimneys (until 1842, girls as well as boys worked down the pits). There was no Poor Law assistance in the industrial towns. The only escape for a respectable girl was to go into **service.** For those who were not respectable there was prostitution, white slavery, prison.

Legal changes

Children: the **Custody of Infants Act** (1839), following a campaign led by Caroline Norton, gave a mother the right of access to her children, in the event of separation; she could be denied access to them unless proved to be of unblemished character. This denial of access on grounds of bad character was ended by an act of 1873.

The Guardianship of Infants Act (1886), allowed a woman to be the sole guardian of her children upon the death of her husband. This act established that children were the property of the mother as well as the father and acts in 1891 and the twentieth century established that a husband had to prove suitability before being given custody of the children.

Divorce became possible by the Matrimonial Causes Act (1857); where hitherto a marriage could only be nullified on grounds of non-consummation, the act set up a Divorce Court which would grant a divorce to a man whose wife had committed adultery, but to a woman only if the husband had been guilty of cruelty or desertion, in addition to adultery. This was a costly procedure which only the prosperous could afford.

It was regarded as a great disgrace to be divorced and it was not until 1887 that Queen Victoria would allow a divorced person, even the innocent party, to attend court.

It was not until 1925 that women could sue for divorce on the same grounds as men.

The property of a woman went to her husband on marriage. This was gradually changed.

The first change came about when the **Matrimonial Causes Act** (1857) allowed women who had lost the protection of their husband, to take legal charge of their own property.

A Married Women's Property Act was passed in 1870, but it was so amended in the House of Lords that it had little impact. The act came fifteen years after a petition with 26 000 signatures, but the idea was condemned as contrary to the law of England and to the law of God. It did however, enable women to keep the first £200 of any money that they earned themselves. In 1882, this was taken a step further and married women obtained the **right to separate ownership** of all kinds of property, thus taking away the husband's automatic right to his wife's property.

Education

An important part in the changing status of women was brought about by improved education for women. This has already been dealt with on pages 71 and 72. The improved education for women also helped to open up new opportunities for them to join the professions and other forms of employment.

Work for women

When, during the Crimean War, **Florence Nightingale** set off with her band of nurses for the base hospital at Scutari, she did more than bring cleanliness and comfort to the wounded; she brought to **nursing** the publicity and impetus that made it an acceptable occupation for the daughters of the middle classes. The interest she raised was harnessed by her foundation of the **St. Thomas' Hospital School of Nursing** in 1858. Nursing came to be looked upon as a great vocation for which a girl had to qualify by years of training. This came to be regulated by the state through the **Nurses' Registration Act** of 1919.

It was not to be expected that able and ambitious young women should be satisfied with the lowly status of nursing, but it was very difficult for a girl to enter the profession of **medicine**. **Elizabeth Garrett** was the first woman doctor in this country, but she had not been able to qualify in this country. Her determination was such that she qualified abroad. This was true of girls wishing to follow her example. The **London School of Medicine for Women** was established in 1872. Medical schools were given the power to examine women students in 1876. In spite of their success, it was not until 1919, when the **Sex Disqualification Removal Act** declared that no-one should be disqualified from holding public office or civil or judicial posts by reason of their sex or the fact of marriage, that women began to compete with men.

It is difficult to say when **teaching** first attracted women to it, as a career but the work of Miss Buss and Miss Beale (pages 70 to 71) opened up opportunities for women who wished to teach in the **state secondary and elementary schools**, while their more academic sisters gradually found acceptance in higher forms of education.

The Civil Service was slow to open the door to women—the first appointment of any importance being that of a woman to be a poor law inspector in 1872, while in 1883 Dilke appointed several women as inspectors for the local government board. Asquith appointed the first women factory inspectors. Such appointments were the exception rather than the rule and it was not until 1921 (two years after the Sex Disqualification Removal Act) that the government accepted a resolution of the House of Commons that women should be admitted to the civil service in Great Britain on the same terms as men.

For daughters of working class parents, perhaps the biggest single factor in freeing them from the sweatshops in the towns, was the invention of the **typewriter** (or the Remington as the first practical model to appear on the market was called). It was the typewriter that opened the doors to a business world for women. By the turn of the century, 9 000 women were employed as office workers and the numbers were increasing rapidly. The invention of the **telephone**, two years later in 1876, by Alexender Graham Bell, led to a further demand for young women in offices to act as telephonists.

The employment of women in many trades, such as **engineering**, hitherto regarded as exclusively male, was an enormous boost to their employment opportunities and to the esteem in which they were held.

Government action in the field of employment for women was slow, but action was taken to prevent the exploitation of women in some industries:

1. **The Coal Mines Act** of 1842 made it illegal to employ female labour down the mines (a prohibition that still stands).
2. **The Factory Act** of 1844 limited women's hours in the mills to 12 per day and prohibited women from cleaning machinery whilst it was in motion.
3. **The Ten Hour Act** of 1847 had to be augmented by acts in 1850 and 1853 before the ten hour day became a reality.

This 'protective' attitude of the government towards women was to show itself from time to time although it was at obvious variance with their refusal to treat them equally. One example of this ambivalent attitude is that when devising the details of the retirement pension, it was decided that women should contribute less and receive less benefit but that they should receive it at the age of 60 instead of 65.

Votes for women

The early victorians mostly agreed with Queen Victoria when she said that, 'We women are not made for governing'. The struggle for women to achieve equality in the field of politics was therefore, more bitter than in other fields.

Millicent Fawcett began to work for the constitutional movement for women's suffrage immediately after her marriage in 1867. She was criticized in parliament after her first meeting for disgracing herself by speaking in public. From that time, with the support of her husband, John Stuart Mill, James Stansfield and other sympathisers, a Woman's Suffrage Bill was introduced almost every year for fifty years, only to be defeated. Her movement was against specific acts of violence and the members preferred to call themselves **suffragists** to distinguish themselves from their more militant sisters the suffragettes.

John Stuart Mill wrote and spoke in the fifties and sixties in support of votes for women. During the debates on Disraeli's Act (1867), Mill proposed that women should be enfranchised; his motion was defeated by 196 votes to 73.

The peacful movements for votes for women, drawn together by **Lydia Beck** in her National Union of Women's Suffrage Societies, created a shift in public opinion in favour of a measure of reform but failed to convince parliament. This led a minority to ridicule the constitutional approach and to adopt militant methods. They ignored the success that had been achieved.

Progress was made in **Local Government**:

By the **Municipal Corporations Act** (1869), women who were householders and unmarried had the right to vote in the Borough council elections.

Similarly, the **County Councils Act** (1888), which gave new elected councils the duties formerly carried out by Justices of the Peace, gave women householders, who were unmarried, the right to vote, in the County council elections.

The **Parish Councils Act** of 1894, which set up Urban and Rural Districts and Parish Councils, gave women, whether married or not, the right not only to vote but also to be members of the new councils. There seemed to be no impediment now to votes for women in general elections.

The suffragettes were determined to gain votes for women by any means available, including violence. They were formed in 1903 as the **Women's Social and Political Union**, by Mrs. Emmeline Pankhurst and her daughters Christabel and Sylvia. They decided that the government needed to be shocked out of their complacency and planned an all-out attack on the newly elected Liberal government in 1906. This was probably a mistake because on the whole the Liberals were well disposed towards them, but were unlikely to act in the face of attacks on their persons and their property.

Their campaign became increasingly militant:

Election meetings were disturbed and members arrested for disturbing the peace. Some elected to go to prison rather than pay the resultant fine.

Public demonstrations were staged.

Processions to parliament organized.

A policy of '**Keep the Liberals out**' was adopted in by-elections. Harassment of leading Liberals led to arrests.

Pamphlets were dropped on London from a balloon.

Emily Davison threw herself under the king's horse in the Derby thereby providing a martyr for the movement.

The tactic of going on **hunger strike** in prison was adopted. The government frightened lest one should die on their hands responded with **forcible feeding**.

Militancy was suspended (1910–1911) while an **all-party Conciliation Committee** tried to agree on a Women's Suffrage Bill. Failure led to increased militancy, with attacks on public and private property and vandalism in art galleries. The government responded with the **Cat and Mouse Act** (1913), whereby women whose health was in danger from forcible feeding could be set free and re-arrested later.

Unfortunately, the leaders of both parties could see political reasons for not giving women the vote.

The Liberals feared that the women, if enfranchised, would respond by voting Unionist.

The Unionists, in the main, were hostile to the idea.

Bills were introduced to give women the vote but none of them reached the statute book before the outbreak of war in 1914.

The First World War brought an end to internal strife: the country turned a united front to the enemy. Women undertook many tasks for the sake of the country. They worked in armament factories; they drove ambulances; they acted as secretaries; they ran canteens; they provided entertainment. At the end of the war, possibly out of respect for women's war work or perhaps to avoid any further confrontation with militant women, the government introduced the **Representation of the People Act** (1918) allowing women who were over 30 years of age, and property owners or married to property owners, the right to vote in parliamentary elections. **Equality with men** was not achieved until the act of 1928 which gave the vote to all women over twenty-one, with the usual exceptions as for men. With women outnumbering men, there were some fears that the nature of elections would change, with domestic and female issues to the fore. In fact there was little change and many women simply voted for the same party as their husbands.

Women and sport

Women were not involved in the so-called national sports of rugby, cricket or football, but with the arrival of **Lawn Tennis** in 1874, women began to play and the first Women's Championship at Wimbledon was held in 1884. Lawn tennis became a feature of week-end parties for the upper and middle classes. It was one of the reasons for a mild pre-occupation with athleticism among young women and it was one of the reasons for the more hampering fashions in women's dress to disappear.

Golf was another sport open to female participation from 1885; it demanded a good deal of physical effort and again led to a demand among women for less restrictive clothes.

Most important of these new sports was the **bicycle**. It became very popular after the invention of the **safety bicycle** in 1886 and the **pneumatic tyre** in 1888. Whether used singly, or as a member of one of the clubs that appeared, it was cheap and it more than doubled the distance which could be covered for an outing or for going to work. It was the fastest thing on the roads and it was very fashionable. Townspeople were able to visit the countryside and the younger housewives in the villages were able to shop in town and go to the theatre, the music hall and the cinema. It led to a decline in the practice of chaperoning young ladies of the upper classes and it increased the mobility, especially of the younger ladies. Though age need be no barrier especially for those like Mrs Bloomer who were able to adopt a more sensible mode of dress for the sport.

Fashion was much affected by sport because of the need for greater freedom of movement:

Crinolines went out of fashion in 1868.

The bustle went out of fashion about 1890 and from about that time the substitution of knickers for thick heavy petticoats made it possible for skirts to be worn shorter so that they no longer swept the ground. This in turn lessened the volume and weight of women's clothes and made it easier for them to move around.

Public Transport as well as the bicycle played its part in making people more mobile.

Cable trams were brought to this country from America in 1884.

Electric trams, largely experimental until 1890, were brought over from Germany.

The South London Tube was opened in 1890 and the Central London Railway in 1900.

Britain took no part in the development of the internal combustion engine, preferring to continue with the practice of having a man with a red flag walking in front of vehicles until 1896. However, after that date a motor car industry did develop.

All of these changes brought a new dimension to the lives of people, including women.

Birth control

There was a slight drop in the birth rate from 1877, when Charles Bradlaugh and Annie Besant were prosecuted for publishing a Malthusian pamphlet which, it is thought, first spread knowledge of birth control in England. This knowledge took time to disseminate, but the middle classes began restricting their families from about this time. With this knowledge, women rebelled against the burden of excessive child bearing. There were economic reasons too for restricting families. Children could no longer be sent out to work at an early age to augment the family income. Rather, compulsory education, even after it was made free in 1891, meant that children were an economic liability at a time when parents were beginning to regard a family less as a life-time's task. They wanted more time and money to spend on what was becoming known as the 'English week-end'.

For most working class women knowledge of birth control methods was not available before the twentieth century.

The Welfare State

The term '**Welfare State**' first appeared in the Oxford English Dictionary in 1955: it meant, 'a state so organized, that every member is assured of his due maintenance, with the most advantageous conditions possible for all'. Although the term is fairly new, the concept is old, going back to the days when the state, in the days of the first Elizabeth, acknowledged by the Poor Law of 1601 that children and orphans, the sick, the aged and the infirm were entitled to the protection of the state. It also asserted that the sturdy beggar must be made to work, if need be, in a House of Correction.

The Elizabethan Poor Law was administered and paid for by the Parish, under the supervision of the Justice of the Peace. In spite of its faults and with the help of certain amending laws and practices, it lasted for 300 years although it had not coped adequately with the strain placed upon it by industrialization and had had to undergo major surgery in the shape of the **Poor Law Amendment Act** of 1834.

During the nineteenth century, there emerged a demand for a more embracing system. This need was urged by working class organizations, by humanitarians, by landowners, by medical men and administrators such as **John Simon** and **Edwin Chadwick**. It should include measures of Public Health, Factory Conditions and Poor Law.

In 1878, the **reverend William Blackley** suggested a scheme of social security, financed on the principle of a compulsory insurance levy, organized through the Post Office.

The work of **Charles Booth**, *Life and Labour of the People of London* (1889) and that of **Seebohm Rowntree**, *Poverty—a Study in Town Life* (1901), coupled with the ideas of a variety of **socialist groups** and individuals put considerable pressure upon the government to accept responsibility for social welfare and to do something about it.

The Conservatives

1897 **A Workmen's Compensation Act** was passed, by which a workman could obtain compensation for injury at work without having to prove negligence on the part of his employer. Certain trades only were included but this was extended by a **Liberal Act** of 1906 to include all trades.

1905 **A Royal Commission** was appointed to study the working of the Poor Law. It established a number of **Labour Exchanges** on a tentative basis a) to help the able bodied poor find work. b) to provide information for employers who needed workers. c) to help workers willing to travel in search of work.

The Liberals

When the Liberals came to power in 1906 they carried this work further and added their own reforming zeal. Their work may be considered under three headings: Help to the Poor; Improvement of Working Conditions; Protection of Children. **Help to the Poor** was aided by the Report of the Royal Commission which the Conservatives had set up in 1905.

The **Old Age Pension Act** (1908) established a weekly pension of up to five shillings per week for individuals over 70, subject to a means test. For a married couple the amount was seven shillings and sixpence, on the principle that two can live more cheaply than one. Recipients had to be British and the pension was non-contributory.

Encouraged by the success of the experimental Labour Exchanges and the minority report of the Royal Commission, Winston Churchill introduced the **Labour Exchange Act** (1909), which set up a network of labour exchanges over the whole country. This came under the direction of **William** (later Sir William) **Beveridge**, who drew upon this experience when formulating his famous Beveridge Plan.

The **National Insurance Act** (1911), set up a scheme of National insurance in two parts. Part 1 introduced a compulsory insurance against **sickness**. Part 2 introduced a compulsory insurance against **unemployment**. Both schemes were contributory and so placed the burden of financing them upon the workers, helped by the employers and the state. The two together form the basis of the health insurance measures of the modern welfare state.

Part 1 of the scheme covered all male and female workers in manual employment and those in non-manual employment earning not more than £160 per annum. A contribution of 4 pence from the worker, 3 pence from the employer and 2 pence from the state (9 pence for 4 pence) was collected each week by means of a stamp stuck on a card. For those not automatically covered by the scheme, benefits could be obtained by voluntary enrolment with contributions which varied according to age on entry. The benefits were for the worker and not his family, with the exception of maternity benefit.

The **benefits** were:
1. Enrolment on a doctor's panel for free **medical attention**.
2. **Sickness benefit** from 5 to 10 shillings per week for men and 3 shillings to 7 shillings and 6 pence for women for a period of 26 weeks.
3. **Disablement benefit** of 5 shillings per week from the 27th week.
4. **Maternity benefit** of 30 shillings.
5. **Hospital services** (free in cases of real poverty, after a means test).

The whole scheme was administered by an **Insurance Committee** in each county or county borough, with **Approved Insurance Societies** paying out the benefits. Many Friendly Societies and Trade Unions became Approved Societies.

Part 2 of the scheme was experimental. At first it applied only to $2\frac{1}{4}$ million workers in industries known to have **periodic unemployment**, such as building, ship-building, mechanical engineering and iron foundries which together amounted to some sixth of the industrial population. Again contributions were made by the worker, the employer and the state: each paying $2\frac{1}{2}$ pence per week.

The **benefit** for the worker, but not for dependants, was at the rate of 7 shillings a week for a maximum of fifteen weeks in any year (unemployment benefit).

There was some **opposition** to the scheme from workers and socialists, who objected to the contributory nature of the scheme, but the main opposition came from the doctors who finally agreed to a capitation fee of 9 shillings.

The act became law in December 1911 and the scheme was in operation by the appointed day (July 15th 1912).

The whole scheme gave the poorer paid workers a **sense of security** in the face of sickness and unemployment which they had never had before, but sickness to any dependant, not covered by the scheme, could still mean real hardship.

It may be noted that increasing unemployment in the period between the wars strained the scheme to its limits. For those outside the scope of the act, there was no help but the old Poor Law, which was still governed by a strict means test.

Improved Working Conditions includes legislation affecting **trade unions** in 1906 and 1913, which has been dealt with in another chapter.

The **Workmen's Compensation Act** of 1906 see page 88.

The **Trade Boards Act** or Sweated Industries Act of 1909 set up Trade Boards with equal representation of employers and workers in those industries such as the small workshops along the High Street where the employees were mostly women without trade union protection, where the government felt that they should intervene to obtain minimum standards of pay and conditions.

The **Shop Hours Act** (1912) was another example of government action in an area where they felt people needed protection. Hours and conditions of shop assistants were regulated and a statutory half day holiday each week laid down. This was in conjunction with the half day early closing day for shops.

The **Coal Miners Minimum Wages Act** (1912) was the first attempt to regulate wages in the mines in its figures for coal-hewing. It was a marked departure from the policy of Laissez Faire on the part of the government.

Protection of Children was an area of considerable activity by the government.

The **Provision of Meals Act** (1906) empowered Local Education Authorities to feed children who came to school hungry. This was an attempt to combat the growing incidence of rickets among school children, due to malnutrition and it shows a growing concern for the physical well being of the nation.

The **Medical Inspection Act** (1907) brought children in elementary schools under medical supervision. The scheme has grown to include children in secondary schools and to include the setting up of special clinics for school children.

The **Children's Charter** (1908) represented an attempt to save young offenders from being brought into contact with hardened criminals. It was hoped that this would increase the chance of reforming these young people. Special, **juvenile courts** were set up where their names need not be disclosed and where the press could be excluded if it was felt that publicity might be harmful.

The **sale of drink and tobacco** (and cigarettes) to young children was forbidden.

Detention in a **Borstal**, approved school or rehabilitation centre was used to keep children out of prisons in the hope of reform rather than retribution.

These Liberal reforms may be said to have laid the foundation of the welfare state that was to be introduced by the Labour Government of 1945. It should perhaps be pointed out that some of these reforms were not new but the product of a long standing concern for children and an extension of services already provided by some authorities.

Transport

Railways

The **first steam locomotive** was built by a Cornishman, Richard Trevithick (1804). Others followed; notably Blackett's 'Puffing Billy' and Stephenson's 'Blucher'. Both of these were used in collieries.

George Stephenson also constructed the **Stockton-Darlington Railway** (1825) as the first public railway using steam locomotives. His '**Rocket**' (1829), reached a speed of 30 m.p.h. on the **Liverpool and Manchester Railway**. He used the 4 ft. $8\frac{1}{2}$ in. gauge used in collieries for his rails.

Stephenson's success encouraged **I.K. Brunel**, the famous engineer of the **Great Western Railway**, who adopted a broad guage of 7 ft.

Railway mania gripped the country in the 1840s. **George Hudson**, the 'railway king' encouraged speculation and amalgamation under his **Midland Railway**. The growth of the railways is shown by the fact that in 1830 there were only 69 miles of track in England, but by 1850, there were 6 621 miles.

Technical improvements such as semaphore and the electric telegraph provided an efficient system of signalling. Old open carriages were replaced and dining and sleeping cars introduced as well as corridor trains.

Railways ended the use of **canals** except for the transport of heavy, durable goods. They developed into an important industry selling British 'know-how' all over the world.

The **Cheap Trains Act** (1844) helped the growth of railways and further simplification came with the abandonment of the wide guage by the Great Western Railway. This helped the amalgamation in the early twentieth century into the '**big four**'—the L.M.S., L.N.E.R., the G.W.R. and the SOUTHERN.

Underground railways developed from 1863, when part of the **Metropolitan Railway** ran underground in London. The **London 'tube'** was opened in 1884 and in 1890 began the first electric railway.

Shipping

Experiments to adapt James Watt's steam engine to water transport began as early as the first experiments with locomotives. The first successful steamship was the '**Charlotte Dundas**' which plied on the Forth and Clyde Canal (1802).

Meanwhile, in the U.S.A., Robert Fulton launched his '**Clermont**' on the Hudson River, successfully using paddles. This practice was copied by Bell in his famous '**Comet**' (1812), which carried passengers on the Clyde.

Many early steam ships used sails as well as steam and it was not until 1833 that the Canadian ship, the '**Royal William**', first crossed the Atlantic entirely under steam. Although paddle-steamers like the '**Great Western**' could cross to New York in eighteen days, they were replaced, after 1840, by the more efficient **screw-propelled steamers**. With the greater efficiency of the **expansion engine**, there was greater economy in the use of fuel and therefore more room for freight or passengers. Screw-propelled iron ships gradually established their superiority over even the best sailing ships.

Air travel

The first step towards flying was taken as early as 1783 when the Montgolfier brothers made their first journey. But to be of use balloons needed to be propelled by an engine. From 1900, when **Count Zeppelin** made his first voyage in a dirigible balloon, much progress was made in experimenting with **airships**. These were used in the First World War and a British airship, **the R34**, crossed the Atlantic in both directions (1919). The disaster of the **R101 (1930)** ended the experiments with airships in this country.

Aeroplanes became possible when the internal combustion engine replaced the heavier steam engine. The American brothers, **Orville and Wilbur Wright** made the first flight (1903). Their machine flew for only half a mile but it encouraged others. It was a Frenchman, **Blériot**, who first flew the Channel (1909) and belatedly a recognized industry grew up in Britain (1911).

The **Royal Flying Corps** and the **Royal Naval Air Service** were formed in 1912 and the use of the aeroplane by both sides, in the First World War, greatly improved their performance and their dependability. By 1919, it was possible to set up the first regular daily passenger service, flying from London to Paris.

Index